The **ORGANIC** Coo

Naturally good food

£2.99
4

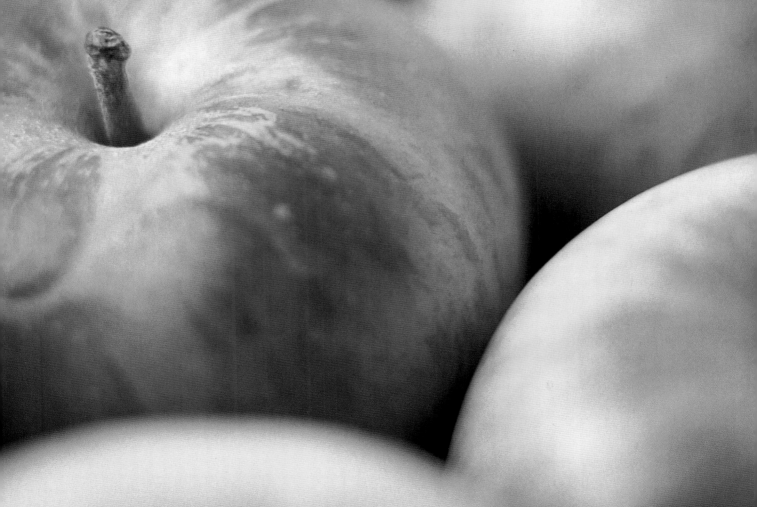

The **ORGANIC**
Cookbook

Renée J Elliott & Eric Treuillé

Photography by Ian O'Leary

A Dorling Kindersley Book

Dorling Kindersley
LONDON, NEW YORK, SYDNEY,
DELHI, PARIS, MUNICH and
JOHANNESBURG

DEDICATION

FROM RENÉE ELLIOTT
To Mom

FROM ERIC TREUILLÉ
This book is dedicated to:
Everyone at Sheepdrove Organic Farm,
but especially Charles Maclean and
Peter Kindersley, for giving me a chance
to participate in a commerical organic
farm in action. Also to Anabel and
Juliet Kindersley, two busy mothers
who garden, shop, cook and eat organic
- these recipes are for you.
And lastly to Eliette Gardou. I grew up
in an intensely rural part of the South
West of France, amongst people deeply
connected to their land and the natural
rhythms of this earth. Most are gone,
but Eliette is still at Le Turelet and
remains my teacher and my inspiration.

First published in 2001
by Dorling Kindersley Pty Limited,
(A.B.N. 42 078 414 445)
118-120 Pacific Highway, St Leonards
NSW 2065

National Library of Australia
Cataloguing-in-Publication data
Elliott, Renée.
The Organic Cookbook:
Naturally Good Food.

Includes index
Hardback ISBN 1-74033-265-2

1.Natural foods. 2. Cookery (Natural
foods). I. Treuillé, Éric.
II Title.

Reproduced in Italy by GRB Editrice,Verona
Printed in Italy by Printer Trento S.r.l.

Printed on acid-free, chlorine-free, recyclable
and biodegradable paper from a sustainable
forestry source.

Organic Cookbook is meant to be used as a
general recipe book and source of information,
not a medical reference book. While every
effort has been made to ensure that the
contents of this book are accurate, it is not
intended to be prescriptive and should in no
way be treated as a substitute or alternative to
qualified medical advice.

www.dk.com

Contents

Foreword

At last! A cookbook that awakens our consciousness to the way we live and the way we eat, to the way food is grown and to the food on our plate. For years I thought I was doing my best by feeding my family fresh vegetables and fruit and whole grains as part of their diet. Then I became involved in biodynamic farming and the certification of biodynamic and organic food, and I found out how many chemicals were used in the conventional growing of our food. Seventeen chemical sprays used to grow a crop of apples, sixteen for strawberries - it sure took the fun out of eating!

No wonder young people no longer eat meat, vegetables and fruit unless they are covered in sauces and marinades! Our food has become so tasteless and bland that it is no longer enjoyed for its flavour. Which is why more and more we are turning to organic and biodynamic produce for healthy food. For optimum health, our food needs to be grown in mineral- and humus-rich soil — organically or biodynamically. This book not only makes you aware of how the food is grown and when to find it at its seasonal best, but also shows you how to select, store and prepare ingredients in order to work with their natural flavour and goodness.

The Certified Organic Food Industry in Australia has been growing at a rate of 20-30% per year. Supermarkets are now carrying organic produce in their fresh vegetable and fruit sections as well as on the dry goods shelves. The Australian organic market is at present valued between $250m and $300m, and there are close to 2,000 certified farmers. By supporting the Certified Organic Industry you are supporting our soils, waterways and our fragile environment, encouraging farmers to look to better ways to grow their crops, and giving yourself and your family a delicious and healthy diet.

Cheryl Kemp
EDUCATION REPRESENTATIVE
ORGANIC FEDERATION OF AUSTRALIA.

Choose Organic

Chefs and food lovers the world over all agree that to cook good food, you have to start with good ingredients.

GOOD FOR YOU
Organic food is good for us, good for our planet and good to eat. Organic cooking begins with organic ingredients, but goes beyond the contents of your shopping basket. To cook organic is more than a buying decision. It is a lifestyle choice, and an attitude that informs the way we cook, eat and shop.

FLAVOUR WITHOUT FUSS
The organic way to cook is about making every ingredient count. The aim is to enhance, not disguise. The better the quality of the ingredients, the less you need to do to them. When you switch to organic ingredients, the much quoted maxim, "keep it simple" is more relevant than ever. For today's time-challenged home cooks, this is good news. Cooking organic means flavour without fuss.

THE SIMPLER THE BETTER
Cooking organic is based on selecting good ingredients and handling them minimally in a way that their distinctive flavour, texture and aroma can be best appreciated. The ingredients are the star and the recipe is their showcase. The simpler, the better. Our recipe selection is intended to reflect this – dishes based on classic combinations and straightforward cooking techniques. Forget time-consuming recipes and multiple "fusion" flavours. Let the ingredients speak for themselves.

RECIPES TO INSPIRE
At every opportunity, we have made our recipes open to adaptation. Often we give a basic recipe with variations that substitute different ingredients but use identical techniques. Alternatively, a recipe is given with a list of the possible ingredients that can be adjusted according to personal preference or availability of ingredients. We suggest alternative ingredients and optional additions to allow the cook to vary a dish according to the season, occasion, mood or simply to what's in the pantry. Recipes are but points of departure. Cooking is a flexible, responsive process; the time, the place and the person all play a role in its special alchemy.

THE NATURAL CHOICE
Organic farming is a carefully defined system of food production, strictly monitored and enforced by law to meet rigorous standards. Organic farmers seek to work with nature rather than control it with chemicals. Organic principles are underpinned by the following:

- *Soil fertility*
- *Free from artificial chemical fertilisers*
- *Free from pesticides*
- *Animal welfare*
- *Free from GMOs*
- *Minimal damage to the environment*
- *Minimal processing and additives*

It is ironic that we refer to the use of chemicals in agriculture as " conventional". Contrary to popular perception, its practice is a wholly new experiment in the history of food production. It is a mere blip in time over the thousands of years since farming began. In reality, it is organic farming, with its combination of modern soil science and traditional, tried-and-tested methods, that is truly the agriculture of today and tomorrow. A sustainable farming system that is free from artificial chemicals produces high-quality food and protects the environment. It is our only option for a future if we are to conserve the earth's precious and finite resources.

GROUND RULES

The secret is in the soil. Intensive farming exhausts the soil, depleting the natural minerals and trace elements essential for nutrient-rich food. For the organic farmer, the soil and its natural fertility are paramount. Various non-artificial methods, such as mixed farming systems that integrate a range of crops with rearing livestock and crop rotation, are used to keep the soil in good health and replace essential nutrients. Appropriate varieties, beneficial predatory insects and companion planting help build resistance to pests and diseases. Naturally strong crops grown in fertile soil will take up a richer nutrient supply. Organic farming delivers healthy soil growing healthy plants producing healthy food.

NATURALLY GOOD TASTE

Organic food is produced as nature intended. Crops and livestock are grown and reared naturally, at their own pace, without artificial fertilisers, synthetic pesticides, chemical feeds, growth-promoting drugs or routine antibiotics. Because organic produce is allowed to develop more slowly, it generally contains less water and more solid matter, which means more nutrients and more flavour. In addition, organic farmers generally favour traditional varieties over modern hybrids and cross-breeds in order to promote biodiversity and to suit climatic conditions. Produce must be harvested at peak condition and transferred from field to store to cooking pot with minimal delay to maintain optimum nutrition and flavour. Industrial food processing and packaging methods can keep produce looking fresh for weeks or even months. Organic crops are not sprayed with post-harvest chemicals to prolong shelf life. Appearances do not deceive, as they do in non-organic produce. Truly fresh food will look, feel, smell and taste fresh.

BUYING ORGANIC, BUYING WHAT'S BEST

This process starts with the shopping basket. The organic cook is an opportunistic shopper who buys what's best on the day. Shop with all your senses. Look, smell, touch, and taste too, if you can, before you buy. Organic ingredients may not be entirely uniform or cosmetically perfect, but, when freshly harvested in their natural season, they have a sheen, a perfume and a vitality that artificially cultivated produce rarely has. Ingredients differ from season to season and day to day, so once in the kitchen, remember to taste before and while you cook.

BE CREATIVE

Remain open to variation and don't be afraid to change seasoning to suit your palate. Cooking is creative, rewarding and fun. Every day, you get to be an artist, inspired by colour, texture, form and aroma, challenged by the blank canvas of a dinner plate. Make cooking pleasurable as well as pleasure-giving.

TASTE AND GOODNESS

Home-cooked food may require more effort than picking up the phone to order a take-away or putting a ready-made meal in the microwave, but the results just don't compare in terms of taste, goodness or enjoyment. Everyone agrees that you are what you eat. Food is our life's sustenance and our first line of defence against disease. When you do the cooking, you're in control. You can ensure optimum nutrition and limit your exposure to the chemicals that non-organic farming practices and food processing methods involve.

RELAX AND NURTURE

As the pace of modern life accelerates ever faster, cooking can be an immensely rewarding and relaxing routine at the end of a challenging day. There are few simple, everyday tasks more satisfying than preparing food for family and friends. The ritual of sitting down together to share a daily meal immeasurably enhances our quality of life. To feed is to nurture and to care for food is to care for ourselves. Eating together is an inclusive experience that nourishes both body and soul. Make time to enjoy it.

Shop with care, cook with pleasure, and eat slowly, in the company of those you love. Respect is at the heart of the organic revolution. Respect for our food, respect for ourselves, and respect for our land - land we hold in trust for future generations.

Choose Seasonal

In the last 30 years, shopping for food has changed dramatically. Seasonal availability has become a thing of the past. We have grown used to having summer berries in winter and spring shoots in autumn. Today, almost any kind of food is available all year round and often at very low prices. But there are hidden costs.

OUT OF SEASON, OUT OF FLAVOUR

Buying food out of season means paying for food that has been picked unripe and transported thousands of miles under controlled atmosphere storage. High yield, cosmetic uniformity, long shelf life and the ability to withstand lengthy transportation are among the commercial criteria that dictate which fruit and vegetable varieties are grown. Taste and goodness are not. The longer the delay between field and plate, the greater the deterioration of flavour and nutrients.

When you buy ingredients in their natural season, they tend to be more plentiful, readily available, reasonably priced and at the peak of flavour and nutrition. A basic knowledge of what is in season is the first step towards top-tasting, nutrient–packed food.

KNOWING WHEN IT'S BEST

The seasonal chart on page 10 is intended as a guide to when fresh produce is at its seasonal peak. We do not suggest that you never again buy the ingredients listed outside of these guidelines. Certain produce does store well and imported ingredients have always played an important role in our culinary traditions. Our aim is to encourage you to seize the opportunity of eating fresh food when it is at its peak and in plentiful supply.

IN TUNE WITH THE SEASONS

It is time for us to renew our link with the rhythms of the natural world. Our bodies hunger for different foods at different times of year – hearty comfort food in the cold winter months, light, refreshing dishes in the summertime – and mother nature matches our moods and supplies our needs. Good produce, like great wine, should speak of the soil, the sun, the rain. The way it tastes will reflect its variety, as well as where it was grown, who grew it, and when it was harvested. All year round availability is limiting our choice and blunting our taste buds with consistently bland food. Shop, cook and eat in tune with the seasons, and the pleasure of eating vegetables and fruits at their appropriate time is yours.

YOU ARE WHAT YOU EAT

Eating a healthy diet is one of the most important things we can do for ourselves. Our bodies are under stress from the fast pace of modern life, yet we live in an increasingly toxic environment, and the food we depend on to nourish and sustain us is treated with artificial chemicals, adulterated with artificial additives and depleted of essential nutrients. Our eating habits have changed drastically over the past twenty years. Food fads, yo-yo dieting and health scares have fostered fear of food and bred ignorance of healthy eating. If we want to eat well, feel good and live better, we need to put home-cooked food made with the best ingredients back on the menu. Vote with your fork – choose organic.

NATURAL SELECTION

The best way to shop for fresh seasonal produce is not to make a list at home, but to wait and see what looks and smells best at the market or store. To preserve maximum flavour and nutrition, store carefully (see pages 12-14) and eat as soon as you can.

Seasonal guide

Hearty Greens & Cabbages

	Spring	Summer	Autumn	Winter
Spinach	● ● ●	● ● ●	● ● ●	●
Swiss Chard	● ● ●	● ● ●	● ● ●	
Spring Greens	● ● ●			● ●
Kale	● ● ●			● ●
Broccoli				
purple sprouting	● ● ●	●		●
Green		● ● ●	● ● ●	● ●
Cauliflower	● ● ●	● ● ●	● ● ●	● ● ●
Cabbages				
Spring Green	● ●	● ●		
Savoy	● ● ●	●	● ● ●	
White	● ●		● ●	● ● ●
Red		●	● ● ●	● ●
Brussel Sprouts				● ● ●
Cavolo Nero				● ● ●

Shoots & Stalks

	Spring	Summer	Autumn	Winter
Asparagus	● ● ●	●		
Globe Artichokes		● ●	● ●	
Fennel	● ●		● ● ●	● ●
Celery	● ● ●	● ● ●	● ● ●	● ● ●

Alliums & Onions

	Spring	Summer	Autumn	Winter
Spring & Salad Onions	● ● ●	● ● ●		
Leeks	● ●	●		● ●
Garlic				
Fresh	● ●	●		
Maincrop		● ● ●	● ● ●	● ● ●
Onions	●	●	● ● ●	● ● ●
Shallots		● ●	● ● ●	● ● ●

Salads & Tender Greens

	Spring	Summer	Autumn	Winter
Watercress	● ● ●	● ●	● ● ●	●
Sorrel	● ● ●	●		
Rocket	● ● ●	● ●	● ● ●	●
Oakleaf		● ●	●	
Romaine		● ●	● ●	
Butterhead Lettuce		●	● ● ●	
Batavia	● ● ●	●	● ● ●	●

Salads & Tender Greens (cont)

	Spring	Summer	Autumn	Winter
Frisée	● ● ●		● ●	● ●
Radicchio	● ●			
Chicory	● ● ●		● ● ●	● ● ●
Mizuna	● ● ●		● ● ●	● ● ●

Fresh Herbs

	Spring	Summer	Autumn	Winter
Parsley	● ● ●	● ● ●	● ● ●	●
Chives	● ●	● ● ●	● ● ●	
Mint	● ●	● ● ●	● ●	
Fennel	●	● ● ●	● ●	
Marjoram		● ● ●	● ● ●	
Oregano		● ● ●	● ● ●	
Tarragon	●	● ● ●	●	
Chervil	●	● ● ●	● ●	
Dill		● ● ●	● ●	
Basil	●	● ● ●	● ●	
Thyme	● ● ●	● ● ●	● ● ●	● ●
Rosemary	● ● ●	● ● ●	● ● ●	● ●
Sage	● ● ●	● ● ●	● ● ●	● ● ●
Bay	● ● ●	● ● ●	● ● ●	● ● ●

Beans & Pods

	Spring	Summer	Autumn	Winter
Broad beans	● ●	● ●		
Peas	●	● ●		
French Beans		● ● ●	●	
Runner Beans		● ● ●	●	
Sweetcorn		● ●	●	

Squashes & Vegetable Fruits

	Spring	Summer	Autumn	Winter
Avocados	● ● ●	● ● ●	● ● ●	● ●
Cucumbers		●	● ● ●	
Summer Squash		●	● ● ●	
Zucchini		●	● ● ●	
Tomatoes		●	● ● ●	
Peppers		● ●	● ●	
Eggplant		● ●	●	
Chillies			●	
Pumpkin			● ● ●	● ● ●
Winter Squash			● ● ●	● ● ●

Roots & Tubers	SPRING	SUMMER	AUTUMN	WINTER
Radishes				
Salad	•••	•••		
Turnips				
Spring	•	•		
Maincrop			•••	••
Carrots	••		•••	••
Potatoes				
New		•••		
Maincrop	••	•	•••	•••
Sweet	•		•••	•••
Beetroot	•	•••		•
Parsnips	•		•••	•••
Celeriac	••		•••	•••
Salsify	••		•••	•••
Swede	•		•••	•••
Jerusalem Artichokes	•		•••	•••
Wild Mushrooms & Fungi				
Morels	••	•		
Chanterelles		•	•••	
Cèpes		•	•••	
Field Mushrooms		•	•••	
Truffles			•	••
Orchard Fruits				
Cherries	•	•••		
Apricots	•	•••		
Peaches		•••	•	
Nectarines		•••	•	
Plums		•••	•••	
Figs		••	•	
Mulberries		•	•	
Pears		••	•••	•••
Apples	•	•	•••	•••
Quinces			•••	
Citrus Fruits				
Lemons	•••	•••	•••	•••
Oranges				
Sweet	•••	••	••	•••
Blood	•••			•••
Seville				••

Citrus Fruits (cont)	SPRING	SUMMER	AUTUMN	WINTER
Grapefruit	•••	••	••	•••
Mandarins	••		••	•••
Kumquats	•		•	•••
Limes		•	•••	•
Vegetable Fruits				
Rhubarb				
Forced	••			••
Outdoor	••	•		
Melons			•••	
Watermelons			•••	
Soft & Vine Fruits				
Strawberries	••			
Raspberries		•	••• •	
Gooseberries			•••	
Currants				
Red & White			••	
Black			••	
Grapes			•••	
Blueberries		••	•	
Blackberries			•••	
Cranberries			•••	••
Tropical Fruit				
Bananas	•••	•••	•••	•••
Pineapples	•••	•••	•••	•••
Papayas	••	•••	•••	•
Mangos		•	•••	•
Passion Fruit	•	•••	••	•
Pomegranates			••	•
Kiwis	•••			•
Dates			•••	•
Persimmons			••	••

BEST BUYS
For optimum, nutrient-packed food, choose locally grown produce in its natural season, especially when there is no organic option on the shelves. When making your buying decisions, let the following criteria guide you to the healthiest choices:

Buy organic
Buy in season
Buy local

SPEAK UP!
What you buy, what you ask for, and what you complain about all play a part in determining the quality and availability of fresh produce in your store. Be prepared to speak up! If they are not selling something, ask for it.

GOODNESS INSIDE OUT
A natural bristle brush is an essential piece of equipment in the organic kitchen. Use it to clean the skins of all fruits and vegetables.

When the peel or skin of fruit and vegetables is edible, leave unpeeled where you can, as the skin and the flesh just beneath the skin are rich in nutrients and fibre. If not organically grown, always peel thoroughly, as even washing with soap or detergent will not remove fungicide and pesticide residues on the skin.

Shop Organic

Good cooking and healthy eating begin with careful shopping and proper storage. Refer to our seasonal chart to get an idea of the seasonal fresh produce you can expect to find in the store. Take time to examine fruit and vegetables before you buy, as their look, feel and smell will tell you a lot about their quality. Get your shopping home without delay, store appropriately and prepare as close to cooking as possible to preserve optimum nutrition. Taste and goodness diminish over time, so the sooner you eat fresh produce, the fuller its flavour and the higher its nutritive value.

Choose fruit and vegetables that look fresh, healthy and 'alive'. Organic produce may not be cosmetically perfect but should not be substandard. Minor blemishes or irregularities are fine, but bruises, soft spots and splits are not. Be prepared to hold, press and sniff as you shop. Fresh produce that is heavy for its size tends to be more succulent and flavourful, while the key to judging ripeness in many fruits and some vegetables is their aroma. A ripe tomato will smell of tomato in a way that a hydroponically-grown tomato never will. Modern houses rarely have cool and airy larders or cold stores. The best option for storing most vegetables and some fruits is in a loosely closed plastic bag with holes pricked in it placed in the vegetable crisper bin of the refrigerator. Always remove from their wrapping any fruit or vegetables that have been sold sealed in plastic or they will sweat and deteriorate.

Hearty greens should look lively and feel squeaky fresh. Any yellowing or limpness indicates age. Spinach is best bought loose, as pre-packed plastic bags often conceal bruised or wilted leaves. Store greens unwashed and refrigerated for up to 4 days.

Choose cabbages with compact heads that feel heavy for their size, and cauliflower or broccoli with tightly formed, crisp looking florets. Refrigerated, cabbages will keep for up to 1 month, cauliflower and broccoli for up to 5 days.

Check the cut ends of shoots such as artichokes and asparagus. If they are brown and dry, they were harvested some time ago. The leaves on artichoke heads and the scales on asparagus tips should be tightly closed like new flower buds, which is essentially what they are. Like flowers, they are best stored with their stems immersed in cold water; refrigerate and cover their tops loosely with a plastic bag. Be sure to first remove any rubber bands from the asparagus stems. Artichokes will keep for up to 1 week. Asparagus are best cooked and eaten on the day of purchase and better still, on the day of harvest.

When selecting vegetable stalks such as celery and fennel look for firm, plump and crisp heads with no signs of browning. In the refrigerator celery keeps well, up to 1 month, while fennel tends to turn dry and fibrous after 5 days.

Dried alliums, such as onions and garlic, store very well, up to 3 months in a cool, dry place. Choose bulbs with dry, papery skins that feel heavy for their size. Reject any that feel light or are starting to sprout.

When choosing fresh alliums, such as leeks and spring onions, look for crisp green tops and firm white bulbs and refrigerate for up to 1 week.

When choosing salad leaves, avoid brown cut ends and wilted or bruised outer leaves. The leaves should be crisp and tightly layered, especially towards the heart. Before storing, always remove and discard damaged leaves. Salad leaves will keep for up to 4 days when refrigerated whole and unwashed and up to 3 days when the leaves are separated, rinsed and dried using a salad spinner. Never tear or cut the leaves until just before serving. To re-crisp limp salad leaves, immerse in icy cold water for 5 minutes, drain and dry in a salad spinner. Chill for 15 minutes in the vegetable crisper bin of the refrigerator before using.

Watercress is best bought in bunches. Untie and pick out any yellowing or wilting sprigs. Store with the leaves plunged down and the stalks up in a jug of cold water in the refrigerator.

Wherever possible, buy herbs in bunches. Store stems down in a jug of cold water loosely covered with a plastic bag; refrigerate for up to 5 days, changing the water every 2 days. Leaves or small sprigs are best stored loosely wrapped in kitchen paper and placed in a loosely closed plastic bag in the refrigerator. Stored in this way, most herbs will keep for up to 4 days, but coriander is best used within 2 days. Select herbs that look lively with no wilted leaves. Your nose is your best guide to fragrant, flavourful herbs.

An easy freshness check for green beans is to fold them in half – they should snap rather than bend. Store refrigerated and use within 5 days. Always buy fresh peas in their pod and shell as close to cooking time as possible. Eat fresh peas without delay as their natural sugars begin to turn to starch after harvesting. Choose shiny, bright green pods that are not too tightly packed, as over mature peas tend to be mealy in texture.

Sweetcorn is also best eaten as soon as possible after harvesting. Always buy corn still in its husks. The husks should be green and moist-looking. To test sweetcorn kernels for freshness, press a kernel with your fingernail. If newly harvested, it should squirt milky juice. Preferably eat fresh peas and sweetcorn on the day of purchase. Otherwise refrigerate and eat the next day.

Vegetable fruits are better not refrigerated as chilling spoils their aroma and texture. A cool, dry room temperature best suits zucchini, squash, tomatoes, avocados and peppers, while even cucumbers do not like excessive cold. A warm kitchen means the vegetable crisper bin of the refrigerator is your only option, but they are still best eaten within 2-3 days of purchase. When making your selection, choose vegetables that are feel firm, look glossy and are heavy for their size. Check the stem end. It should be fresh-looking rather than dried out. To test avocados for ripeness, hold one in the palm of your hand and squeeze very gently; if it yields slightly to pressure, it is ready to eat, otherwise leave to ripen at room temperature or in a closed brown paper bag. Whole winter squashes will keep well for several months in a cool dry place. Once cut, press cling film on to the cut surface and refrigerate for up to 1 week.

Avoid roots that are limp or wrinkled. When you can, buy them with their greens still attached. Greens are a good sign of freshness. If they are healthy and moist-looking, the roots will be too. To store, cut off any greens, leaving a little stalk, and refrigerate unwashed for up to 2 weeks. Beetroot and turnip greens are also good to eat; store and cook as for hearty greens. Potatoes are best stored in a cool, dry place protected from the light in brown paper bags or cloth sacks where they will keep for 2-3 weeks. Avoid any that are sprouting or cracked or that have soft spots or green patches.

Mushrooms should smell pleasantly earthy. Reject any that are withered or slimy. Store loosely packed in brown paper bags so that they can breathe. Refrigerate, but not in the vegetable crisper bin, which is too moist. Use within 3 days.

For top flavour and fragrance, most fruits are best stored at room temperature. Apples, citrus fruits, kiwi fruit and bananas are good keepers and make the best possible fruit bowl staples, but most fruit, once ripe, should be eaten without delay. One-stop, once-weekly shopping trips are not compatible with good fruit eating. To ripen under-ripe fruit, place in a closed brown paper bag, taking care not to overcrowd.

As a general rule, choose fruits that look plump, feel firm and are heavy for their size. Smell, usually at the stalk end, is the best indication of ripeness. Always check delicate fruits such as berries, figs and stone fruits carefully for signs of dampness or bruising. If you do need to keep these more perishable fruits when ripe, store in a loosely closed plastic bag in the vegetable crisper bin of the refrigerator, where they will keep for up to 3 days. If you prefer your melon and pineapple chilled, be sure to store in a closed plastic bag as their scent is invasive and will flavour all your dairy products!

Organic pantry

Keeping a well-stocked pantry is the first step to making home cooking easy. Having basic necessities to hand means a simple meal can be on the table without a shopping trip – a far healthier and cheaper alternative to buying take-away and convenience foods. One word of warning: don't forget that out of date means out of taste and out of goodness. The shelf life of packaged goods may be longer, but it is not indefinite. Oils turn rancid, dried beans and grains go stale and just because an ingredient is in the freezer doesn't mean it will last forever. Here is a list of essential staples, useful stand-bys and a few extra treats.

IN THE KITCHEN CUPBOARD

Black peppercorns – a pepper grinder is an essential tool for all home cooks.

Canned beans – wherever possible, choose beans canned in pure water. Chickpeas are well suited to canning. Use to make sustaining soups, nutty salads, and whiz in a food processor with garlic, lemon and olive oil to taste, for a quick-fix dip.

Chocolate – guilt-free indulgences (in moderation of course!) are an essential part of our organic ethos - happy people live longer! Organic chocolate is, quite simply, more chocolatey, with a higher cocoa butter solids content and no hydrogenated fats.

Dried fruit – enjoy as chewy, energy-giving sweet treats or in winter compôtes for breakfast and dessert.

Dried herbs – not all herbs are worth buying dry, but oregano, thyme, rosemary and *herbes de provence* bring a taste of the sun to soups, stews and marinades.

Dried pulses – lentils are the most useful variety to have on hand as they require no soaking and can be prepared and ready to eat within 20-40 minutes.

Flour - got eggs and milk? With flour as well, crepes or pancakes are just a mix away for simple sweet or savoury snacks or meals. Also useful to have on hand for cakes and pastry. If you only use infrequently, store in the freezer. This will double its lifespan.

BULK BUYS

Buying food loose from bulk bins makes perfect sense. You are paying for the food itself, not the packaging, and you can buy as little or as much as you require. The only drawback when buying loose is that it's up to you to keep track of the use-by date. To avoid spoiling good cooking with stale ingredients, store staples in airtight containers in a cool, dark place, do not mix newly purchased ingredients with those already in the pantry, and follow these storage guidelines:

Use grains within 6 months
Use dried beans and pulses
  within 1 year
Use flour within 2 months
Use nuts within 1 month
Use brown rice within 6 months
Use white rice within 1 year

FREEZING TIPS

Freeze only top-quality fresh foods as soon as possible after purchase. Wrap and pack food carefully to avoid freezer burn. Defrost overnight in the refrigerator. Be sure to label and date all food clearly, and follow the guidelines below on recommended freezing times.

Bread - up to 3 months
Butter - up to 6 months
Fish - up to 3 months
Shellfish - up to 3 months
Meat joints - up to 6 months
Minced or small pieces of meat -
  up to 3 months
Sausages - up to 3 months
Chicken - up to 3 months
Vegetables - up to 1 year
Berries - up to 1 year
Nuts - up to 6 months

Garlic – if you have olive oil, salt, garlic and pasta in the house, you have a meal. We can't imagine a kitchen without this essential ingredient.

Grains – a wealth of healthful grains are availbale organic. We favour cous-cous, polenta or coarse cornmeal and rice - arborio for risotto, basmati for Asian-style dishes, and brown for maximum nutritional value.

Honey – nature's own sweetener. Organic is the superior choice as most commercial honeys have been blended, filtered and heated to high temperatures.

Mustard – use in dressings, sauces and marinades and as a condiment. Creamy Dijon is our preference.

Oils – we like to keep two grades of olive oil to hand - regular extra virgin for cooking and a premium quality extra virgin for dressing, drizzling and dipping. Keep a neutral tasting oil such as sunflower, safflower or grapeseed for stir-frying and for making light dressings.

Olives – for instant nibbles with drinks.

Onions – an essential kitchen staple that is the basis of most good savoury cooking and, when roasted (see page 110) stands alone as a vegetable in its own right. We like to have red as well as yellow in store. Red have a milder flavour and pretty colour.

Pasta – the ultimate staple ingredient for simple sustaining supper fare. Choose Italian and stock a selection of shapes and sizes.

Peanut butter – who could be without it? Choose stone-ground for fullest flavour.

Pesto – use to sauce pasta, enrich vegetable soups and stews, and as a topping for grilled chicken, meat or fish. Refrigerate after opening.

Porridge oats – still the best way to start a cold winter's day.

Salt – food lovers know that the quality of salt matters. Choose good quality sea salt which is unrefined, from unpolluted sources and harvested using traditional methods. We like to keep natural coarse and fine salt to hand.

Shoyu – Japanese soy sauce. Sweeter, lighter and less salty than regular soy.

Spices – the ideal is to buy spices whole and to crush them to order as this allows them to keep their fragrance and flavour longer. Alternatively, renew your supply every six months. Our essentials for the spice pantry are crushed chilli flakes, paprika, cumin, coriander, turmeric, cinnamon and nutmeg.

Tapenade – to spread on bruschetta (see page 54) for an easy opener. Refrigerate after opening.

Tinned tomatoes – whole plum tomatoes are better value and needn't be messy to chop when you know how. Open the tin and snip the tomatoes into pieces with a pair of kitchen scissors. Essential for making pasta sauces and for brightening up winter soups and stews.

Tomato ketchup – a family necessity. Organic ketchups are all-natural, taste more of real tomatoes and are less cloyingly sweet.

Vinegar – red wine and balsamic are basic necessities for all food lovers. Red wine vinegar is the king of French dressings. A drizzle of balsamic vinegar adds depth of flavour to grills and roasts both pre and post cooking.

Wine – make deliciously simple sauces for meat by adding half a glass to the pan after frying. Cook down the pan juices until syrupy. Also essential for slow-cooked stews and braises, and of course for a glass as you cook.

IN THE REFRIGERATOR

Butter – keep your main supply in the freezer for optimum freshness and the purest flavour.

Cheese – PARMESAN stores well in a piece that weighs no more than 250 - 300g (8-10oz), wrapped in foil and kept in the warmest part of the refrigerator. Combined with butter, black pepper and pasta, parmesan provides a simple supper solution. A hard cheese that melts well, such as CHEDDAR or GRUYERE is also a must-have. Cut into dice, it will add richness to winter vegetable soups and sustenance to a crisp green leaf salad. When grated, it is a perfect partner to eggs, especially omelettes or scrambled.

Eggs – the ultimate in convenience food. A few eggs combined with a couple of pantry staples will give you a meal in minutes.

Greens – whether hearty or tender, try to always have something green to hand.

Lemons – as organic lemons are not waxed or treated with post harvest sprays, it is important to store them in the refrigerator. Lemon wedges are the freshest of natural garnishes for simple grilled chicken, meat or fish.

Mayonnaise – a sandwich essential. Organic mayos are made with real eggs, pure oil and natural seasonings only.

Milk – whether cow's or soy, a pantry is not stocked without it.

Natural yoghurt – for breakfast or desserts, or for a low-fat creamy garnish in soups or with pastries. Creamy Greek-style is our favourite.

IN THE FREEZER

Berries – buy in bags or freeze your own at peak season. Great for smoothies, sorbets, fruit fools and quick-fix sauces (see page 116).

Bread – sliced for toast and smaller whole loaves like baguette or ciabatta for putting straight into the oven from the freezer and serving warm.

Butter – cut into conveniently sized pieces, we favour 125g (4oz) pieces, and wrapped airtight.

Ginger – stock up on organic fresh ginger when you can. Cut off chunks, peel and grate frozen as needed.

Ice-cream – with no artificial flavourings or additives, organic ice-cream is the next best thing to home-made. For impromptu desserts, with or without quick-fix sauces (see page 116).

Nuts – pine nuts, almonds and walnuts or pecans get our vote. Their shelf life is limited so we prefer to freeze them. Toast nuts in a dry pan over medium low heat until golden and serve as nutty nibbles, use to add crunch to salads or sprinkle over honey-drizzled yoghurt.

Peas – make a classic pasta sauce with butter as well as children's favourite green vegetable. Always choose *petis pois*.

Sausages – stock up on best quality sausages when you can.

Spinach – your green leaf fix on ice. Bags of loose frozen leaves are our preference.

Soups for all Seasons

SERVES 4

3 tbsp extra virgin olive oil

2 slices streaky bacon, chopped, optional

1 medium onion, finely chopped

2 stalks celery, diced

1 carrot, diced

4 garlic cloves, finely sliced

¼ tsp finely chopped fresh rosemary or a pinch of dried, crumbled rosemary

1 medium potato, diced

300g (10oz) greens (see opposite), coarsely chopped

400g (14oz) tin italian plum tomatoes, chopped

400g (14oz) tin beans (see opposite), drained and rinsed

1.5l (2½ pints) chicken or vegetable stock

salt, black pepper

additional extra virgin olive oil to drizzle

4 tbsp freshly grated parmesan to serve

Tuscan Vegetable Soup with Greens and Beans

• Heat the oil in a heavy-based pot. Add the bacon, if using, onion, celery, carrot, garlic, rosemary, potato and greens. Cook, stirring frequently, over medium low heat until the onions soften and the greens wilt, 10 minutes.

• Turn the heat to medium. Add the tomatoes and cook, stirring occasionally, until just thickened, 10 minutes. Add the beans and stock. Bring to a boil.

• Adjust the heat, partially cover and simmer gently until the vegetables are very tender, 30 minutes. The soup should be fairly thick, but be prepared to add water to thin if necessary. Add salt and pepper to taste. Ladle into warm bowls. Drizzle with oil and sprinkle with parmesan. Serve hot.

VARIATION

Provençal Vegetable Soup with Greens and Beans

Make the soup as directed, adding a small handful of broken up spaghetti to the soup 10-12 minutes before the end of simmering time. Simmer until the pasta is tender. Remove the soup from the heat and stir in 4 tbsp basil pesto. Ladle into warm bowls and serve hot.

WHICH GREENS?

Choose from kale, savoy cabbage, swiss chard, sprouting broccoli, spring greens or cavolo nero.

WHICH BEANS?

You can be equally inspirational about your choice of bean in this soul-satisfying soup. For a delicate flavour and creamy texture, choose from cannellini, haricot or flageolet beans.

For a firmer bite and a slightly nutty taste, choose either borlotti beans or chickpeas.

Potato, Garlic and Parsley Soup

- Heat the oil or butter in a heavy-based pot. Add the potato slices, onion and garlic. Cook, stirring occasionally, over medium heat until the onions are softened, 10 minutes.
- Add half the chopped parsley and the stock. Bring to a boil. Adjust the heat, partially cover and simmer gently until the potatoes are tender, 30 minutes. Add the remaining parsley.
- For a creamy soup, leave to cool slightly and purée until smooth with a hand blender or in a food processor. Alternatively, leave the soup chunky. Stir in the milk or cream, if using. Thin with water as needed. Add salt and pepper to taste. Ladle into warm bowls and serve hot.

VARIATIONS

Potato, Garlic and Leek Soup

Omit the parsley and replace half the potatoes with 3 medium, finely sliced leeks. Cook as directed.

Potato, Garlic and Fennel Soup

Omit the parsley and replace half the potatoes with 2 medium, finely sliced fennel bulbs. Cook and finish as directed.

SERVES 4

2 tbsp extra virgin olive oil or 30g (1oz) butter
750g (1½ lb) potatoes, quartered and finely sliced
1 onion, finely chopped
8 garlic cloves, finely sliced
2 handfuls fresh parsley, chopped
1.5l (2½ pints) chicken or vegetable stock
125ml (4floz) milk or double cream, optional
salt, black pepper

COOK'S TIP

Organic fresh parsley - especially flat-leaf - is not always easy to find. Luckily, it freezes well; chop and store in an airtight container and scoop out straight from the freezer as needed.

HEALTH BITE

Parsley tastes good, looks good and is good for you! This herbal superfood is rich in vitamins A and C as well as calcium, iron and folic acid. Parsley should be added at the end of the cooking time to preserve both its vivid green colour and its optimum nutritional value.

SERVES 4

2 tbsp olive oil
  or 30g (1oz) butter
1 large onion, finely chopped
4 garlic cloves, crushed
2 tbsp freshly grated ginger
1 tsp ground cumin
1 tsp ground coriander
¼ tsp cayenne pepper
750g (1½ lb) carrots, roughly
  chopped
1 medium potato, roughly
  chopped
1.5l (2½ pts) chicken
  or vegetable stock
1 tsp honey
2 tbsp lemon or orange juice
salt, black pepper

HEALTH BITE
Chock-full of beta carotene,
carrots really are good for your
eyesight. They also cleanse,
alkalize, nourish and stimulate
many body systems, while sup-
plying a great-tasting, easy-to-
digest dose of vitamins and
minerals.

Moroccan Spiced
Carrot Soup

• Heat the oil or butter in a heavy-based pot. Add the onion, garlic, ginger, cumin, coriander, cayenne, carrot and potato and cook, stirring occasionally, over medium low heat until the vegetables are soft, 10 minutes.
• Turn the heat to medium. Add the stock and bring to a boil. Adjust the heat, partially cover and simmer gently until the potato is tender, 30 minutes.
• Leave to cool slightly. Purée until smooth with a hand blender or in a food processor. Stir in honey and lemon or orange juice. Thin with water as needed. Add salt and pepper to taste. Ladle into warm bowls and serve hot.

VARIATION
Carrot and Parsnip Soup with Ginger
Omit the cumin, coriander and cayenne. Replace half the carrots with 2 chopped medium parsnips. Cook as directed.

Pick-Me-Up
Miso Tofu Soup

- Place the miso in a bowl and stir in a little of the water to dilute to a thick cream. Set aside.
- Place the remaining water in a pan and bring to a boil. Lower the heat and add the tofu, mushrooms and carrots. Simmer gently until the tofu rises to the surface, 3 minutes.
- Remove from the heat and stir in the diluted miso. Ladle into warmed bowls and sprinkle with spring onions and sesame oil. Serve hot.

WHICH MISO?

Miso is available in many varieties that vary in colour, texture and saltiness, but basically divides into 2 types. Red miso is thicker and saltier and is traditionally used in winter soups. White miso is more delicate and sweeter, and is preferred for lighter, summer soups.

SERVES 4

3 tbsp miso (see opposite)
1 l (1¾ pints) water
75g (2½ oz) firm tofu, diced
4 button mushrooms, finely sliced
½ carrot, cut into fine matchsticks
2 spring onions, finely sliced
a few drops toasted sesame oil

HEALTH BITE

Miso is a protein-rich fermented soy bean paste. Considered in Japan as a gift from the gods, it has readily digestible amino acids, fatty acids and simple sugars. Never boil miso, as boiling destroys its living enzymes.

Roast Red Pepper and Tomato Soup with Basil

SERVES 4

2kg (4¼ lb) ripe tomatoes, halved

2 red peppers, cored, seeded and quartered

2 red onions, quartered

1 handful fresh basil, leaves and stalks torn

4 garlic cloves, crushed

1 tbsp balsamic vinegar

4 tbsp extra virgin olive oil

¼ tsp crushed chilli flakes

salt, black pepper

extra torn fresh basil leaves to serve

COOK'S TIP

Both peppers and tomatoes are best stored at room temperature, as refrigeration spoils their texture and aroma.

HEALTH BITE

The bright red or orange colour of fruits or vegetables generally indicates high beta-carotene and vitamin C content, and red peppers and ripe tomatoes are no exception to the rule.

• Preheat oven to 200°C (400°F) Gas 6.

• Place the tomatoes cut side up with the peppers and onions in a roasting pan. Scatter with basil. Combine garlic, vinegar and oil and drizzle over the tomatoes, peppers and onions. Sprinkle with chilli flakes, salt and pepper. Roast until very soft and wilted, 1 hour.

• Leave to cool slightly. Purée, leaving a little texture, with a hand blender or in a food processor. The soup should be fairly thick, but be prepared to thin with water if necessary. Add salt and pepper to taste. Ladle into warm bowls and sprinkle with extra basil. Serve hot or at room temperature.

Spiced Green Lentil Soup with Spinach and Lemon

SERVES 4

2 tbsp extra virgin olive oil
1 onion, finely chopped
4 garlic cloves, crushed
3 celery stalks, diced
2 medium potatoes, diced
1 tsp ground cumin
250g (8oz) green lentils
1.5l (2½ pints) chicken or
  vegetable stock
500g (1lb) spinach or swiss
  chard, coarsely chopped
2 tbsp lemon juice
salt, black pepper

• Heat the oil in a heavy-based pot. Add the onion, garlic, celery, potato and cumin and cook, stirring frequently, over medium low heat until the potato is tender, 10 minutes.

• Increase the heat to medium. Add the lentils and stock and bring to a boil. Adjust the heat, partially cover and simmer gently until the lentils are tender, 20-30 minutes.

• Add the spinach or chard and cook until wilted but still bright green, 3 minutes. Add the lemon juice and salt and pepper to taste. Ladle into warm bowls and serve hot.

HEALTH BITE
An essential part of any health-smart diet plan, lentils are high-protein, high-fibre and iron-rich. They are also an excellent source of valuable B vitamins.

VARIATION

Hearty Green Lentil Soup with Bacon and Red Wine Vinegar

Omit the ground cumin. Add 4 chopped streaky bacon slices with the onion, celery and potato to the pot. Cook as directed. Replace the lemon juice with 1 tbsp red wine vinegar.

Ginger Squash Soup

SERVES 4

2 tbsp sunflower oil

1kg (2lb) orange-fleshed winter squash or pumpkin, peeled, seeded and cut first into wedges and then into chunks

1 medium potato, quartered and finely sliced

1 medium leek, finely sliced

4 garlic cloves, crushed

2 tbsp freshly grated ginger

1.5l (2½ pints) vegetable stock or water

lemon or lime juice to taste

salt, black pepper

COOK'S TIP

Look for squashes that are heavy for their size, with thick, hard skins showing no blemishes or bruises. In general, the harder the skins, the riper - and sweeter - the squash. Winter squash store well, and in fact generally improve after a few weeks of storage.

HEALTH BITE

The most medicinal of spices, ginger is an aromatic stimulant and is thought to promote overall circulation of energy in the body. It can also aid digestion, ease nausea and fight coughs and colds.

• Heat the oil in a heavy-based pot. Add the squash, potato, leek, garlic and ginger and cook, stirring occasionally, over medium heat until the vegetables are soft, 10 minutes.

• Add the stock and bring to a boil. Adjust the heat, partially cover and simmer gently until the potato is tender, 30 minutes.

• Add lemon or lime juice and salt and pepper to taste. Ladle into warm bowls and serve hot.

VARIATIONS

Ginger Squash Soup with Lemon Grass and Coconut

Add the finely chopped tender stem of 1 lemon grass stalk to the pot with the vegetables and cook as directed. When the vegetables are tender, stir in 125ml (4floz) tinned coconut milk. Heat through and proceed as directed.

WHICH SQUASH?

Butternut or hubbard squash would be our preference, but any squash with deep orange flesh will be rich in flavour.

Whole Meal Salads

Crisp Leaf Salad with Apple, Blue Cheese and Walnuts

• For the dressing, mix together vinegar and oil until blended. Add salt and pepper to taste.

• Place the walnut pieces in a dry pan over a medium heat. Toast, shaking the pan occasionally, until browned, 5 minutes. Remove from the pan and leave to cool.

• Place the salad leaves, apple and cucumber in a large bowl. Add dressing and toss to coat. Arrange on a serving dish or plates. Sprinkle with walnuts and cheese. Serve immediately.

VARIATION

Bitter Leaf Salad with Pear, Blue Cheese & Walnuts

Omit the crisp salad leaves and replace with 4 handfuls bitter leaves, such as frisée, chicory, batavia, watercress or rocket. Omit apples and replace with 2 pears. Omit cucumber and replace with 1 fennel bulb. Proceed as directed.

Mozzarella, Tomato and Avocado Salad with Basil

• Layer the tomatoes, avocado and mozzarella on a large serving dish or individual plates, sprinkling with salt and pepper in between the layers. Drizzle over lemon juice and oil. Scatter with basil and serve immediately.

SERVES 4
FOR THE DRESSING
2 tbsp red wine vinegar
4 tbsp extra virgin olive oil
salt, black pepper

60g (2oz) walnut pieces
4 handfuls crisp salad leaves such as cos, little gem or iceberg, torn
2 apples, cut into 2cm (¾ in) pieces
1 cucumber, cut into 2cm (¾ in) cubes
125g (4oz) blue cheese, crumbled

HEALTH BITE
The king of fruit and great detoxifiers, apples are loaded with pectin, a soluable fibre that sweeps toxins out of the body. They are also potassium rich and highly alkaline. An apple a day really can help keep the doctor away!

SERVES 4
4 ripe tomatoes, sliced
2 avocados, halved and sliced crosswise
250g (8oz) mozzarella, sliced
salt, black pepper
1 tbsp lemon juice
3 tbsp extra virgin olive oil
1 handful fresh basil leaves, torn

COOK'S TIP
Never store ripe tomatoes in the refrigerator, as this spoils their texture and aroma. It is far better to eat them immediately, at the height of their ripeness, freshness and goodness.

HEALTH BITE
Eaten raw, ripe and fresh, tomatoes are a powerhouse of vitamin C. They are also rich in lycopene, an antioxidant that assists in preventing heart disease and cancer.

Grilled Vegetable Platter with Pesto Dressing

• For the dressing, place the pine nuts or almonds in a dry pan over medium heat. Toast, stirring frequently, until golden and fragrant, 10 minutes. Remove from the pan immediately and leave to cool. Place pine nuts or almonds, basil or parsley, garlic and oil in a food processor; pulse until smooth. Add salt and pepper to taste.

• Preheat a barbecue grill or ridged cast-iron grill pan to medium hot.

• Brush the vegetables with olive oil and sprinkle with salt and pepper. Grill, turning once or twice, until lightly charred and tender.

• Toss with pesto dressing. Arrange on a large serving dish. Serve hot or at room temperature.

WHICH VEGETABLES?

Tender summer vegetables are best for grilling. Choose from:

red, yellow or orange peppers, quartered
tomatoes, ripe, firm and halved
eggplant, cut into 1cm (½in) thick rounds
red onions, cut into 2cm (¾in) thick rounds
zucchini, cut lengthwise into 1cm (½in) thick slices
asparagus, woody end snapped off
spring onions, whole
summer squash, cut into wedges

SERVES 4

FOR THE PESTO DRESSING
2 tbsp pine nuts or almonds
2 handfuls fresh basil or
   flat-leaf parsley
1 garlic clove, crushed
6 tbsp extra virgin olive oil
salt, black pepper

1kg (2lb) mixed vegetables
   (see opposite)
extra virgin olive oil
salt, black pepper

COOK'S TIP
You can grill the vegetables up to 6 hours in advance. Cover and store at room temperature. Refrigeration spoils their smoky flavour.

SERVES 4
FOR THE DRESSING
1 tsp grainy dijon mustard
1 tsp horseradish sauce
1 tsp sugar
2 tbsp white wine vinegar
4 tbsp extra virgin olive oil
salt, black pepper

1 bunch watercress
2 heads chicory, separated
  into leaves
½ red onion, finely sliced
175g (6oz) smoked salmon
black pepper

HEALTH BITE
Like other dark green leafy vegetables, watercress is rich in
anti-carcinogenic antioxidants.

Watercress, Chicory and Smoked Salmon Salad with Horseradish Dressing

• For the dressing, mix together the mustard, horseradish, sugar, vinegar and oil until thick and smooth. Add salt and pepper to taste.
• Place the watercress, chicory and red onion in a large bowl. Add the dressing and toss to coat. Arrange on a serving dish or plates. Lay the salmon slices on top. Sprinkle with pepper. Serve immediately.

VARIATION
Watercress and Chicory Salad with Smoked Trout
Replace smoked salmon with 2 fillets of smoked trout, flaked. Proceed as directed.

French Lentil Salad with Baby Spinach

- Place the lentils in a large pan with cold water to cover by 5cm (2in). Bring to a boil. Adjust heat and simmer until the lentils are tender, 20-30 minutes.
- Drain and place the lentils in a large bowl with the garlic, mustard, vinegar, oil and onion. Mix well. Add salt and pepper to taste. Just before serving, add parsley and spinach and toss to combine. Serve warm or at room temperature.

VARIATION
French Lentil Salad with Bitter Leaves

Omit baby spinach leaves and replace with 2 heads chicory, leaves separated, or 1 medium radicchio, leaves torn into bite-sized pieces, or 4 handfuls frisée, torn. Proceed as directed.

Bacon, Avocado and Goat's Cheese Salad with Dijon Dressing

- Preheat the oven to 180°C (350°F) Gas 4.
- For the dressing, mix together mustard, vinegar and olive oil until thick and smooth. Add salt and pepper to taste.
- Place the bacon on a foil-lined baking sheet. Cook until crisp and golden, 10-15 minutes. Drain on kitchen paper. Using kitchen scissors, snip the bacon into 2cm (¾in) pieces.
- Place the bacon, spinach and avocado in a large bowl. Add the dressing and toss to coat. Arrange on a serving dish or plates. Top with goat's cheese. Serve immediately.

SERVES 4

250g (8oz) puy or green lentils
2 garlic cloves, crushed
1 tsp creamy dijon mustard
2 tbsp red wine vinegar
4 tbsp extra virgin olive oil
1 small red onion, finely sliced
salt, black pepper
2 tbsp chopped fresh parsley
4 handfuls baby spinach leaves, washed

COOK'S TIP
You can cook lentils up to 1 day in advance, but for maximum flavour, be sure to dress them while they are still hot. Cover and refrigerate, but return to room temperature before serving. Puy lentils are the best choice for salads as they hold their shape when cooked.

SERVES 4
FOR THE DRESSING
2 tsp creamy dijon mustard
2 tbsp balsamic vinegar
4 tbsp extra virgin olive oil
salt, black pepper

12 slices streaky bacon
4 large handfuls baby spinach leaves, washed
2 avocados, quartered and sliced
125g (4oz) goat's cheese, diced

COOK'S TIP
There is no need to restrict this salad to baby spinach. Crisp salad leaves are also delicious. Tear into bite-sized pieces.

HEALTH BITE
Easily digestible, with a perfect pH balance, avocados are packed with minerals that regulate body function.

Roast Pepper, Artichoke and Feta Salad with Rocket

SERVES 4

2 red peppers
1 small red onion, finely sliced
1 – 300g (10oz) jar artichoke hearts in oil, drained and quartered
4 tomatoes, quartered, seeded and halved
125g (4oz) feta cheese, diced
1 tbsp capers, drained and rinsed
4 handfuls rocket
1 tbsp brown rice vinegar
3 tbsp extra virgin olive oil
salt, black pepper

COOK'S TIP

You can roast and peel the peppers up to 3 days in advance. Cover and refrigerate, but return to room temperature before serving. Although peppery rocket is our preference, other salad greens work well. Try sprigs of fresh flat-leaf parsley or watercress, or tear salad leaves into bite-sized pieces.
You can assemble and dress the salad up to 1 day in advance, but add the rocket just before serving.

• Roast the peppers under a hot grill, turning as needed, until charred and wrinkled on all sides, 10-15 minutes. Place in a plastic bag or a bowl with a plate on top and leave until cool. The steam released by the peppers as they cool will loosen the skin.
• Uncover the cooled peppers. Peel off the charred skin, scraping off any remaining bits of skin. Cut the peppers into quarters and remove the core. Scrape away the seeds and discard. Cut the quarters into 2.5cm (1in) pieces.
• Place the pepper, onion, artichoke hearts, tomatoes, feta, capers, rocket, vinegar and oil in a large bowl. Toss to coat. Add salt and pepper to taste. Serve immediately.

ROAST PEPPER SALAD ADD-ONS
Add 2 tbsp black olives to the salad. Finish as directed.

Pizza, Focaccia & Bruschetta

Olive Oil Rich **Dough**

• Place the flour and salt in a large bowl. Make a well in the centre and add the water. Sprinkle over the yeast and leave to stand until softened, 5 minutes. Stir to dissolve.

• Draw in flour from the sides to make a sticky dough. Turn out on to a lightly floured surface. Knead to a smooth, soft dough. Try not to add too much extra flour, as the dough will firm up as you knead it.

• Place the dough in an oiled bowl and cover. Leave to rise until doubled in size, about 1-1½ hours. Deflate the dough by pressing down with the palm of your hand. The dough is now ready for shaping into pizza bases (see below) or focaccia (see page 53).

Pizza Bases

• Divide the dough into 4 equal-sized pieces. Shape each piece into a ball, cover with a cloth and set aside for 10 minutes. This allows the dough to rest, making it easier to stretch. The shaped dough balls can stand covered with a cloth for up to 1 hour before shaping, topping and baking.

• Place a dough ball on a lightly floured surface. Roll out the dough with a rolling pin to a 30cm (12in) round about 5mm (¼in) thick. Turn the dough over several times as you roll it, to prevent it from sticking or shrinking. If the dough resists stretching, leave it to rest again for 3 minutes. Don't worry if the dough is not perfectly round.

• Dust a baking sheet with coarse cornmeal. Place a shaped dough round on the dusted baking sheet.

MAKES ENOUGH DOUGH FOR 4 PIZZAS OR 1 FOCACCIA
400g (14oz) strong white flour, additional for dusting
1 tsp salt
250ml (8floz) tepid water
1 tsp dried active yeast
1½ tbsp olive oil

COOK'S TIP
The dough will be quite sticky but try to resist working in too much extra flour as you knead. A moist dough bakes to a light pizza base with a crisp crust and an airy crumb, while a stiff dough willl make heavy bases.

MAKES 4 - 30cm (12in) PIZZA BASES
1 recipe olive oil rich dough (see above)
flour and coarse cornmeal for sprinkling

Spinach, Blue Cheese and Pine Nut **Pizza**

• Adjust your racks to the top of the oven. Place pizza stone or baking sheet in the oven and preheat the oven to as hot as possible, allowing 30 minutes.

• For the tomato sauce, place the tomatoes and their juice in a food processor; pulse until smooth.

• If using fresh spinach, rinse well. Place in a large pan with the water still clinging to the leaves. Cook over high heat, stirring frequently, until wilted and bright green, 3-5 minutes. Drain and rinse in cold water. With your hands, squeeze spinach to remove excess water.

• Shape one pizza and place on a dusted baking sheet (see page 47). Spread pizza base evenly with tomato sauce. Cover with an even layer of spinach. Sprinkle with blue cheese, pine nuts, salt and pepper. Drizzle over oil.

• Slide the pizza off the baking sheet onto the stone, if using, or onto the preheated baking sheet in the oven (see cook's tip). Bake until the crust is crisp and golden, 5-10 minutes. Serve immediately.

• Repeat with the remaining toppings and pizzas.

MAKES 4 PIZZAS
FOR THE PIZZA
1 recipe olive oil rich dough (see page 47)
coarse cornmeal for sprinkling

FOR THE TOMATO SAUCE
400g (14oz) tin italian plum tomatoes, whole not chopped

FOR THE TOPPING
750g (1½ lb) fresh spinach, or 300g (10oz) frozen spinach, defrosted and squeezed dry
200g (7oz) blue cheese, preferably gorgonzola, crumbled
4 tbsp pine nuts
salt, black pepper
2 tbsp extra virgin olive oil

COOK'S TIP
We highly recommend using a pizza stone or a preheated heavy baking sheet. A stone provides an intense heat to cook the crust quickly and evenly.
To transfer the pizza to the stone with ease, make sure you dust the baking sheet with enough cornmeal. Shake the sheet back and forwards in order to loosen and to allow the pizza to slide off easily. If it doesn't slide off, remove and dust again. Place the edge of the baking sheet on to the edge of the stone. With a sharp yank, pull away the baking sheet from under the pizza.

Grilled Eggplant Pizza with Basil

MAKES 4 PIZZAS

1 medium eggplant, cut into 5mm (¼ in) thick slices

2 tbsp extra virgin olive oil, plus additional for brushing and drizzling

2 garlic cloves, crushed

1 recipe olive oil rich dough (see page 47)

½ medium red onion, finely sliced

125g (4oz) mozzarella, finely sliced

2 ripe tomatoes, cut into 5mm (¼ in) thick slices

salt, black pepper

1 handful fresh basil leaves, torn

COOK'S TIP

For the crispest crusts, it's best to bake the pizzas one at a time. When the first pizza is in the oven, start topping the second, so, when the first is ready to eat, the second will be ready to bake. Then, by the time you have finished eating the first, the second will be ready. Pizza is best eaten as soon as it comes out of the oven as the crust will soften as it cools.

• Adjust your racks to the top of the oven. Place pizza stone or baking sheet in the oven and preheat the oven to as hot as possible, allowing 30 minutes.

• Preheat a ridged cast-iron grill pan or overhead grill. Brush the eggplant slices on both sides with olive oil. Grill until lightly charred and tender, 5 minutes per side.

• Combine the garlic and the oil.

• Shape one pizza and place on a dusted baking sheet (see page 47). Brush one pizza base with garlic oil.

• Arrange red onion slices, mozzarella slices, eggplant slices and tomato slices in a even layers over the pizza base. Sprinkle with salt and pepper. Drizzle over a little oil.

• Slide the pizza off the baking sheet onto the stone, if using, or the baking sheet in the oven (see cook's tip on page 49). Alternatively, place the baking sheet on a rack in the oven. Bake until the crust is crisp and golden, 5-10 minutes. Serve immediately.

• Repeat with the remaining toppings and pizzas.

VARIATION

Red Pepper and Oregano Pizza

Omit eggplant, tomatoes and basil. Replace with 2 red peppers cut into fine strips. Combine the pepper strips, red onion slices, crushed garlic, 2 tbsp oil and salt and pepper to taste. Arrange mozzarella over one pizza base in a single layer. Spread pepper mixture evenly over the mozzarella. Sprinkle over a pinch each dried oregano and crushed chilli flakes. Bake as directed. Scatter with basil and serve immediately. Repeat with the remaining toppings and pizza bases.

Simple Olive Oil Focaccia

- Press the dough into the oiled oven tray. Dimple the dough all over with your fingertips, making dents 1cm (½in) deep. Cover with a cloth and leave to rise until doubled in thickness, 45 minutes.
- Preheat the oven to 200°C (400°F) Gas 6.
- Sprinkle the dough with salt and bake until golden and hollow-sounding when tapped underneath, 30 - 40 minutes. Drizzle over the additional oil. Cool on a wire rack.

VARIATIONS

Rosemary Focaccia

Follow recipe for dough on page 47, adding 2 tsp finely chopped fresh rosemary or 1 tsp crumbled dried rosemary to the flour with the salt. Proceed as directed. Just before baking, decorate the focaccia with fresh rosemary leaves.

Olive Focaccia

Follow recipe for dough on page 47, kneading 150g (5oz) pitted black or green olives into the dough towards the end of kneading. Proceed as directed.

Onion Focaccia

Cut 1 halved onion into very fine slices. Scatter the shaped dough with onion slices. Proceed as directed.

MAKES 1 FOCACCIA
1 recipe olive oil rich dough (see page 47)
1 tsp coarse salt
2 tbsp additional extra virgin olive oil

ESSENTIAL EQUIPMENT
33cm x 23cm (13 x 9in) oven tray

COOK'S TIP
You can bake the focaccia up to 1 day in advance. Leave to cool completely before storing in a loosely closed plastic bag at room temperature. Warm through in a preheated 150°C (300°F) Gas 2 oven for 15 minutes before serving.

Olive Oil Bruschetta with Red Pepper and Almond Pesto

SERVES 4

FOR THE PESTO
2 large red peppers
50g (1¾ oz) almonds
2 garlic cloves
¼ tsp crushed chilli flakes
½ tsp balsamic vinegar
4 tbsp extra virgin olive oil
salt, black pepper

FOR THE BRUSCHETTA
4 slices day-old bread, cut
  into 1cm (½ in) thick slices
1 garlic clove, halved
extra virgin olive oil

COOK'S TIP
You can make the pesto up to 3
days in advance. Cover and
refrigerate, but return to room
temperature before serving.

• Roast peppers under a hot grill, turning as needed, until charred and wrinkled on all sides, 10-15 minutes. Place in a plastic bag or a bowl with a plate on top and leave until cool. The steam released by the peppers as they cool will loosen the skin. Uncover the cooled peppers. Peel of the charred skin, scraping off any remaining bits of skin. Cut the peppers into quarters and remove the core. Scrape away seeds and discard.
• Place the almonds in a dry pan over medium heat. Toast, stirring frequently, until golden and fragrant, 10 minutes. Remove the almonds from the pan immediately. Place the roast peppers, garlic, almonds, chilli flakes, vinegar and oil in a food processor; pulse until smooth. Add salt and pepper to taste.
• To make the bruschetta, toast the bread on a preheated ridged cast-iron grill pan or barbecue until crisp and striped, 2 minutes per side. Alternatively, use a preheated overhead grill. Rub one side of each slice with the cut garlic and drizzle over olive oil.
• Spread the pepper and almond pesto over the bruschetta. Serve at room temperature.

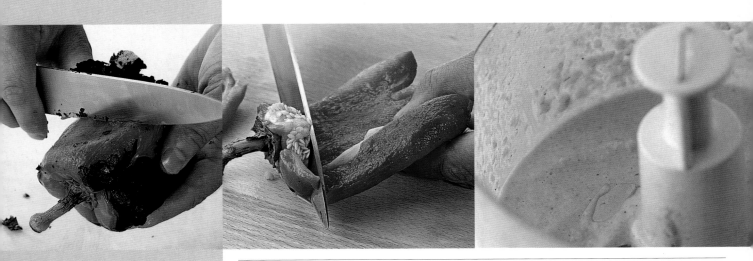

SERVES 4

FOR THE BRUSCHETTA

4 slices day-old bread, cut
   into 1cm (½ in) thick slices
1 garlic clove, halved
extra virgin olive oil

MORE TOPPINGS FOR OLIVE OIL BRUSCHETTA

Bruschetta with Avocado Goat's Cheese

Prepare avocado yoghurt dressing (see page 108), replacing yoghurt with 125g (4oz) fresh creamy goat's cheese. Make bruschetta as directed on page 54. Spread avocado goat's cheese over the bruschetta. Serve at room temperature.

Bruschetta with Roast Cherry Tomatoes

Prepare 1 recipe Roast Cherry Tomato Sauce (see page 68). Make bruschetta as directed on page 54. Spread tomatoes over the bruschetta. Serve at room temperature.

Bruschetta with Marinated White Beans

Prepare 1 recipe Marinated Beans with Olive Oil, Lemon and Chilli (see page 101). Mash the beans with a wooden spoon to make a rough purée. Make bruschetta as directed on page 54. Spread bean mixture over the bruschetta. Serve at room temperature.

Bruschetta with Pan-Fried Mushrooms

Prepare 1 recipe Pan-Fried Mushrooms (see page 60). Make bruschetta as directed on page 54. Spread mushrooms over the bruschetta. Serve immediately.

What's for Dinner?

Polenta

SERVES 4
FOR THE POLENTA
850ml (1½ pints) water
175g (6oz) polenta or coarse
   cornmeal
1 tsp salt
½ tsp black pepper

COOK'S TIP
You can make the polenta up to 3
days in advance. Wrap in cling
film and refrigerate.

- Bring the water to a boil in a heavy-based pot. Turn heat to medium and gradually pour in the polenta, stirring constantly. Add salt and turn heat to low. Cook, stirring constantly, until the polenta is very thick and pulls away from the sides of the pot, 15 minutes.
- Add pepper and mix-ins (see below), if using. Pour the hot polenta onto an oiled baking sheet and spread into a round about 30cm (12in) in diameter and 1cm (½in) thick. Leave to cool until set.

POLENTA MIX-INS
For added flavour, stir in any or a combination of 2 crushed garlic cloves, 4 tbsp freshly grated parmesan, 2 tbsp chopped fresh herbs, such as parsley, basil, thyme or rosemary.

SERVES 4
FOR THE MUSHROOMS
2 tbsp extra virgin olive oil
2 shallots
1 garlic clove, chopped
500g (1lb) mushrooms,
   shiitake, field, chestnut,
   oyster or any combination
125ml (4floz) crème fraîche
   or double cream

1 recipe polenta (see above)
30g (1oz) butter

Crisp Polenta with Pan-Fried Mushrooms

- Preheat an overhead grill.
- Heat the oil in a heavy frying pan. Add shallots, garlic and mushrooms and cook, stirring constantly, over high heat until mushrooms wilt and start to crisp, 5 minutes. Add crème fraîche or cream and cook until just thickened, 2 minutes.
- Cut the polenta into 8 wedges. Dot the wedges with butter. Grill until crisp and golden, 5-10 minutes. Serve immediately with the hot mushrooms.

SERVES 4
1 recipe polenta (see above)
30g (1oz) butter
4 tbsp freshly grated
   parmesan
200g (7oz) blue cheese,
   preferably gorgonzola,
   crumbled

Crisp Polenta with Blue Cheese and Butter

- Preheat an overhead grill.
- Cut the polenta into 8 wedges. Dot the wedges with butter and sprinkle with parmesan. Grill under a preheated overhead grill until crisp and golden, 5-10 minutes. Sprinkle with gorgonzola and serve immediately.

Pan-Roast Chicken with Herbed Goat's Cheese

SERVES 4

125g (4oz) fresh creamy
  goat's cheese
2 tbsp finely chopped
  fresh herbs (see opposite)
1 garlic clove, crushed
salt, black pepper
4 boneless chicken breasts
  (with skins)
2 tbsp extra virgin olive oil

COOK'S TIP

You can prepare the chicken
breasts up to 1 day in advance.
Wrap in cling film and refrigerate.
If possible, leave to stand at room
temperature for 20 minutes before
cooking.

• Preheat the oven to 200°C (400°F) Gas 6.

• Combine the goat's cheese, herbs and garlic. Add salt and pepper to taste.

• With one hand on a chicken breast to hold it in place, slice through the middle horizontally to cut almost in half. Open out flat. Spread a quarter of the herbed mixture over the opened out breast. Fold over and secure by threading a bamboo skewer or toothpick through the cut edges of each breast. Repeat with the remaining chicken breasts and herbed mixture.

• Heat the oil in an oven-proof heavy frying pan or cast-iron ridged grill pan. Add the chicken skin-side down and cook over medium heat until lightly golden, 5 minutes. Turn the chicken skin side up. Sprinkle with salt and pepper.

• Place the pan in the oven. Roast the chicken until cooked through, about 10 minutes. Serve hot on warmed plates with Parsley Smashed Potatoes (see page 94) and Slow-Roast Tomatoes (see page 100).

WHICH HERBS?

Vary the fresh herb according to what is available. Choose any one or a combination of parsley, basil, chives, thyme, spring onions, oregano, tarragon, watercress or rocket.

French Leek Tart

- Preheat the oven to 180°C (350°F) Gas 4.
- Place a baking sheet in the oven to preheat.
- Melt the butter in a large frying pan over a medium low heat. Add the leeks and cook, stirring frequently, until very soft and wilted, 20-30 minutes. Leave to cool slightly.
- Beat the eggs, crème fraîche or cream, salt, pepper and nutmeg until well combined. Add the cooled leeks to the egg mixture. Spread mixture over the pre-baked pastry case. Place tart in the oven on the preheated baking sheet.
- Bake until the tart is golden and just set, 30 minutes. Leave to cool on a wire rack for 10 minutes before serving. Cut into wedges and serve hot, warm or at room temperature.

VARIATIONS

Onion Tart

Replace leeks with 4 large or 6 medium onions, finely sliced. Cook as directed for leeks. Add to the egg mixture and proceed as directed.

Spinach Tart

Replace leeks with 1kg (2lb) spinach. Rinse spinach. Place in a large pan with the water still clinging to the leaves. Cook over high heat, stirring frequently, until wilted and bright green, 3-5 minutes. Drain and rinse in cold water. With your hands, squeeze spinach to remove excess water. Chop coarsely. Add to the egg mixture with 125g (4oz) grated parmesan, gruyère or cheddar cheese. Proceed as directed.

Broccoli Tart

Replace leeks with 500g (1lb) broccoli, stems finely sliced and florets separated. Steam over boiling, salted water until the stems are tender, 12-15 minutes. Leave to cool. Add the broccoli and 125g (4oz) grated parmesan, gruyère or cheddar cheese to the egg mixture and proceed as directed.

Mushroom Tart

Replace leeks with 500g (1 lb) sliced brown or field mushrooms and 1 finely chopped onion. Heat 2 tbsp oil in a heavy frying pan. Add the mushrooms and onion and cook, stirring constantly over high heat, until wilted and starting to crisp, 5 minutes. Remove from the pan and leave to cool. Add to the egg mixture and proceed as directed.

SERVES 4-6
FOR THE FILLING
60g (2oz) butter
4 large leeks, finely sliced
2 eggs, beaten
250ml (8floz) crème fraîche
  or double cream
1 tsp salt
½ tsp black pepper
¼ tsp grated nutmeg
1 - 25cm (10in) pastry case,
  pre-baked (see page 66)

COOK'S TIP
You can bake the tart up to 1 day in advance. Wrap in cling film and refrigerate. For optimum flavour and texture, warm through in a 150°C (300°F) Gas 2 oven for 15 minutes before serving.

HEALTH BITE
If you are feeling calorie-conscious, replace 125ml (4floz) crème fraîche or double cream with milk or sour cream. For a more indulgent tart, replace the double cream or crème fraîche with mascarpone.

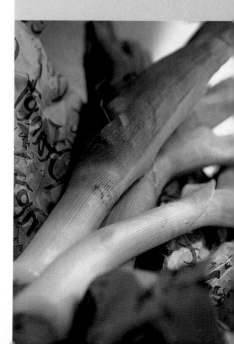

65

Perfect Pastry

MAKES 1 - 25cm (10in) PASTRY CASE

175g (6oz) plain flour
¼ tsp salt
90g (3oz) chilled butter, cubed
1 egg yolk
2 tbsp cold water

ESSENTIAL EQUIPMENT

1 - 25cm (10in) tart tin with a removable base
Baking beans (bought ceramic beans, or dried chickpeas)

COOK'S TIP

You can make the pastry up to 2 days in advance. Wrap in cling film and refrigerate, but be sure to return to room temperature before rolling out. Alternatively, line the tart with pastry up to 1 day in advance and refrigerate or freeze.

• Place the flour, salt and butter in a food processor; pulse until the mixture resembles fine crumbs. Add the egg yolk. Pulse until the pastry draws together, adding the water, ½ tbsp at a time, as needed. Turn out the pastry on to a lightly floured surface and knead briefly to make a smooth round.

• Alternatively, make the pastry by hand. Place the flour, salt and butter in a bowl. With 2 knives, cut the butter into the dry ingredients until the mixture resembles fine crumbs. Add the egg yolk and mix with a wooden spoon until the pastry draws together, adding the water, ½ tbsp at a time, as needed.

• Turn out the pastry on to a lightly floured surface and knead briefly to make a smooth round.

• On a lightly floured surface, roll out the pastry to a 3mm (⅛in) thickness. To line the tin, roll the pastry loosely around the rolling pin, then lift it and unroll carefully over the tart tin. Gently press the pastry over the base and up the sides of the tin. Use pastry scraps to patch any tears. Trim the edges of the pastry, letting it come up just above the sides of the tin. Chill or freeze for at least 15 minutes, to allow the pastry to relax in order to minimize shrinking.

• Preheat the oven to 200°C (400°F) Gas 6.

• Line the tart shell with baking parchment and fill with baking beans. Bake until the pastry is firm, 10 minutes. Remove the paper and beans. Continue baking until crisp and golden, 10 minutes. If not filling and baking immediately, leave to cool on a wire rack.

Roast Cherry Tomato
Spaghetti

- Preheat the oven to 200°C (400°F) Gas 6.
- In a roasting pan, combine the cherry tomatoes, garlic, chilli flakes, oil and vinegar. Sprinkle with salt and pepper. Toss well to coat. Roast until soft and wilted, 20 minutes.
- Cook the pasta in a large pot of boiling, salted water until firm to the bite. Drain well and return pasta to the warm pot with the roast tomato sauce and basil, if using. Toss well to coat. Serve hot on warmed plates.

VARIATION
Roast Cherry Tomato Spaghetti with Goat's Cheese
Cook the tomatoes and pasta as directed. Toss 125g (4oz) crumbled fresh creamy goat's cheese together with the pasta and the sauce.

Slow-Simmered Tomato Pasta Sauce

- Place the tomatoes, garlic and oil in a deep frying pan over medium heat. Bring to a boil. Adjust the heat and simmer slowly, stirring occasionally, until thick, 30 minutes. Add salt and pepper to taste.
- Cook the pasta in a large pot of boiling, salted water until firm to the bite. Drain well and add pasta to the hot sauce. Toss well to coat. Serve hot on warmed plates, with parmesan.

VARIATION
Slow-Simmered Tomato Pasta Sauce with Molten Mozzarella
Cook tomatoes and pasta as directed. Add 125g (4oz) diced mozzarella to the pasta and the sauce.

SERVES 4

500g (1lb) cherry tomatoes
1 garlic clove, crushed
¼ tsp crushed chilli flakes
4 tbsp extra virgin olive oil
1 tbsp balsamic vinegar
salt, black pepper
500g (1lb) spaghetti
1 handful fresh basil leaves, optional

COOK'S TIP
If you can't find cherry tomatoes, use 8 fresh ripe tomatoes cut into equal-sized chunks.

HEALTH BITE
Pasta is great food for keeping our motors running. Its slow release of carbohydrates can keep energy levels high for hours.

SERVES 4

2 - 400g (14oz) tins italian plum tomatoes, chopped
6 garlic cloves, crushed
6 tbsp extra virgin olive oil
salt, black pepper
500g (1lb) penne
freshly grated parmesan

COOK'S TIP
Make the sauce up to 3 days in advance. Cover and refrigerate.

HEALTH BITE
Tomatoes are an excellent source of lycopene, an antioxidant that has been shown to help reduce the risk of certain types of cancer. Recent research has shown that tinned tomatoes contain even higher levels of lycopene than fresh tomatoes.

Coriander Roast Lamb with Spiced Chickpea Sauce

- Place the coriander, cumin, allspice, cinnamon, onion, garlic, tomato, lemon juice and oil in a food processor; pulse to a smooth paste.
- Use a small, sharp knife to cut small slits in the lamb. Push some of the coriander mixture into the slits. Rub the lamb all over with the remaining coriander mixture. Marinate for up to 1 hour at room temperature, or up to 4 hours in the refrigerator.
- Preheat the oven to 200°C (400°F) Gas 6.
- Rub the lamb all over with salt and pepper. Place in a roasting pan. Roast until medium rare, about 1 hour. Cover loosely with foil and leave to rest for 10 minutes before carving.
- While the lamb is roasting, make the spiced chickpea sauce. Place chickpeas, garlic, cumin, tabasco, lemon, tahini, water and yoghurt in a food processor; pulse until smooth. Add salt and pepper to taste.
- Carve lamb and serve hot on warmed plates with the spiced chickpea sauce.

VARIATION

Balsamic Roast Lamb with Garlic and Rosemary

Omit the coriander mixture. Replace with 6 crushed garlic cloves, 1 tbsp finely chopped fresh rosemary, 2 tbsp balsamic vinegar and 2 tbsp olive oil. Mix garlic, rosemary, vinegar and oil to a paste. Proceed as directed.

Omit Spiced Chickpea Sauce. Serve with Marinated White Beans with Olive Oil, Lemon and Chilli (see page 101).

SERVES 4 - 6

1½ tsp ground coriander
½ tsp ground cumin
¼ tsp ground allspice
¼ tsp ground cinnamon
1 onion, chopped
4 garlic cloves, chopped
1 ripe tomato
2 tbsp lemon juice
2 tbsp olive oil
1 leg of lamb, weighing about 2kg (4¼ lb)
2 tsp salt, 1 tsp black pepper

FOR THE SPICED CHICKPEA SAUCE
400g (14oz) tin chickpeas, drained and rinsed
2 garlic cloves, crushed
½ tsp ground cumin
¼ tsp tabasco
2 tbsp lemon juice
5 tbsp tahini
5 tbsp water
125ml (4floz) greek-style yoghurt
salt, black pepper

COOK'S TIP
Lamb takes about 15 minutes per 500g (1lb) to roast to medium rare at 200°C (400°F) Gas 6, so, if your leg of lamb weighs any more or less than 2kg (4¼ lb), calculate the cooking time accordingly.

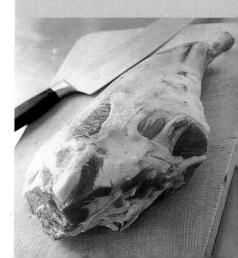

SERVES

4 pork chops, about 2.5cm
(1in) thick
1 tbsp sunflower oil
30g (1oz) butter
2 apples, cut into 8 wedges
4 shallots, halved but still
attached at the root end
1 garlic clove, crushed
125ml (4floz) dry cider
salt, black pepper

Pan-Fried Pork Chops with **Golden** Shallots and Cider Apple **Sauce**

• Trim off excess fat from the chops. With scissors, cut snips through the remaining fat at 4cm (1½in) intervals.

• Heat the oil in a large frying pan over high heat. Add the chops to the pan and cook until golden brown, 2 minutes per side. Reduce heat to low, cover the pan and cook until there is no trace of pink near the bone but the pork is still moist and juicy, about 5 minutes per side. Remove the chops from the pan to a warmed dish. Cover with foil and keep warm in a 120°C (250°F) Gas ½ oven while you make the sauce.

• Turn the heat to medium high and allow the pan juices to reduce and caramelize, 2 minutes. Add the butter to the pan. Add the apples and shallots and cook, stirring occasionally, until soft and golden brown, 8 minutes. Add the garlic and cider and bring to a boil. Cook, stirring and scraping the bottom of the pan, until reduced by half, 3-5 minutes. Add salt and pepper to taste.

• Arrange the chops on warmed plates and sprinkle with salt and pepper. Arrange shallots and apples on top and spoon over pan juices. Serve hot with Mustard Smashed Potatoes (see page 94).

Olive Oil Braised
Mediterranean Vegetables

SERVES 4 AS A MAIN

4 tbsp extra virgin olive oil
1 medium onion, finely
  chopped
2 celery stalks, finely
  chopped
1 medium carrot, finely
  chopped
4 garlic cloves, crushed
½ tsp crumbled dried
  rosemary or 1 tsp finely
  chopped fresh rosemary
½ tsp crushed chilli flakes
1 medium eggplant, cut
  into 1cm (½ in) cubes
2 medium zucchini, cut
  into 1cm (½ in) cubes
2 red peppers, cored, seeded
  and cut into 1cm (½ in)
  cubes
2 potatoes, cut into 1cm
  (½ in) cubes
4 ripe fresh tomatoes or
  tinned plum tomatoes,
  quartered
125ml (4 floz) water
400g (14oz) tin white beans,
  drained and rinsed
1 handful fresh basil, mint
  or parsley or a combination,
  chopped
salt, black pepper
additional extra virgin olive oil
  to serve

• Heat the oil in a large pot. Add the onion, celery, carrot and garlic and cook over medium heat, stirring constantly, until soft, 5 minutes. Add the rosemary, chilli flakes, eggplant, zucchini, peppers, potato, tomatoes and water. Turn the heat down to low and cover. Cook gently, stirring occasionally, until very soft, 30 minutes.

• Stir in the beans and cook until hot through, 5 minutes. Add the herbs and salt and pepper to taste. Serve hot in warmed bowls, drizzled with olive oil.

VARIATION
Olive Oil Braised Winter Vegetables
Replace eggplant, zucchini and red pepper with 750g (1½lb) squash, cut into chunks, 2 leeks, thickly sliced, and 2 fennel bulbs, roughly chopped. Proceed as directed.

Perfect Roast Chicken with Green Olives and Lemon Roast Potatoes

- Preheat the oven to 200°C (400°F) Gas 6.
- Smear the chicken all over with oil and rub with salt. Put a pinch each of salt and pepper inside the cavity, together with the olives.
- Combine the potato quarters with the garlic, lemon juice, oil, rosemary, salt and pepper. Mix well to coat each potato quarter evenly. Choose a roasting tin that will just accommodate the chicken and the vegetables. Place the chicken in the pan and surround with the potatoes.
- Roast the chicken for 1½ hours, basting every 20 minutes, until golden brown with a crisp skin. To test for doneness, stick a fork into the chicken under the wing and hold up the chicken, cavity down. If the juices run clear, not pink, it is cooked through. Remove from the oven and leave to rest for 10 minutes to allow the juices to settle.
- Carve and serve hot with the warm green olives, crisp garlicky potatoes and chicken juices.

SERVES 4 - 6
1 - 1.5kg (3lb) chicken
3 tbsp extra virgin olive oil
2 tsp salt
black pepper
150g (5oz) green olives

FOR THE POTATOES
1kg (2lb) potatoes,
  quartered lengthwise
2 garlic cloves, crushed
juice of 1 lemon
3 tbsp extra virgin olive oil
2 tsp finely chopped fresh
  rosemary or ½ tsp crumbled
  dried rosemary
1 tsp coarse salt
½ tsp black pepper

COOK'S TIP
This roast chicken carcass will make a wonderful stock. Place the bones in a pan and add cold water to cover. Bring to a boil, reduce heat and simmer for at least 2 hours, adding water if necessary to keep the bones covered. Strain stock into a large bowl and refrigerate. Once the stock has set, you can remove the layer of fat from the top.

SERVES 4 - 6

1kg (2lb) piece beef suitable for stewing, braising or pot-roasting, such as topside, silverside or brisket

2 tsp black pepper

2 garlic cloves, finely chopped

1 onion, finely chopped

4 streaky bacon slices, finely chopped

½ tsp dried thyme or 1 tsp fresh thyme

4 carrots, cut into 8cm (3in) lengths

4 celery stalks, cut into 8cm (3in) lengths

8 shallots or 2 onions, root end intact, peeled and quartered

8 whole garlic cloves

12 brown or field mushrooms

8 medium potatoes, halved lengthwise

250ml (8floz) red wine

2 tbsp cognac or brandy, optional

salt, black pepper

COOK'S TIP

This recipe is the ultimate in hands-off cooking. You don't even have to brown the meat and vegetables. Just place everything in the pot and cook very slowly while you get on with something else.

HEALTH BITE

Research shows that red wine in moderation may lower the risk of heart disease. Now that's news to drink to!

Slow-Simmered Beef Daube with Red Wine and Garlic

• Preheat the oven to 150°C (300°F) Gas 2.

• Sprinkle the beef all over with black pepper. In a heavy-based pot, place the garlic, onion, bacon and thyme. Place the beef on top and surround with the carrots, celery, shallots or onions, garlic, mushrooms and potatoes. Pour over the red wine and cognac, if using. Place the pot over medium heat and bring just to a simmer. Cover and put into the oven to cook slowly until very tender, 3-4 hours, making sure that the liquid does not boil. Add salt and pepper to taste.

• Cut the beef into thick slices and place on warmed plates. Surround with the vegetables and spoon over the beef juices. Serve hot.

VARIATION

Slow-Simmered Beef Stew with Red Wine and Garlic

Use stewing beef cut into 4cm (1½in) cubes in place of the whole piece of beef. Heat 1 tbsp olive oil in the cooking pot and fry meat a few pieces at a time until browned all over, 3 minutes. Remove from pot and proceed as directed.

Best Sausages with Golden Onions, Red Peppers and Tomatoes

SERVES 4
8 best pork sausages, pricked
2 onions, finely sliced
2 red peppers, cored, seeded and cut into fine strips
400g (14oz) tin italian plum tomatoes, chopped
salt, black pepper
1 handful chopped fresh parsley, optional

• Heat a large frying pan over medium heat. Add the sausages and cook until browned all over, 8-10 minutes. Remove from the pan and set aside.
• Add the onions to the pan, cover with a lid, and cook until soft and wilted, 5 minutes. Remove the cover and stir in the pepper strips. Cook, stirring frequently, until the onion is golden and the pepper tender, 10 minutes. Add the tomatoes and cook, stirring occasionally, until thickened, 10 minutes.
• Turn the heat to low and return the sausages to the pan. Cook, stirring occasionally, for a further 10 minutes. Add salt and pepper to taste. Serve hot on warmed plates, sprinkled with parsley, if using.

VARIATION
Best Sausages with Golden Onions, Cabbage & Tomatoes
Omit red peppers. Replace with ½ savoy or white cabbage, cored and shredded. Cook as directed.

SERVES 4
8 lamb rib or loin chops
2 garlic cloves, crushed
2 tsp black pepper
½ tsp dried thyme or
1 tsp fresh thyme leaves
1 tbsp balsamic vinegar
1 tbsp extra virgin
   olive oil
salt
lemon wedges

SERVES 4 AS A MAIN, 6 AS A SIDE
FOR THE DHAL
30g (1oz) butter
1 onion, finely chopped
1 garlic clove, finely chopped
1 tbsp freshly grated ginger
250g (8oz) red lentils
½ tsp turmeric
725ml (1¼ pints) water
salt

FOR THE AROMATICS
30g (1oz) butter
½ tsp crushed chilli flakes
3 bay leaves
½ tsp cumin seeds
½ tsp fennel seeds
2 garlic cloves, finely
   chopped

COOK'S TIP
You can cook the dhal up to 1 day in advance. Cover and refrigerate. However, for fullest flavour, add the sizzling and fragrant aromatics to the hot dhal just before serving.

HEALTH BITE
High-fibre and low in fat, lentils are also an excellent source of protein, especially when eaten with rice. Rice and lentils combined make up all 8 essential amino acids, so this traditional Indian staple of rice with dhal is the perfect protein provider.

Pan-Grilled **Balsamic** Lamb Chops

• Rub the chops with garlic, pepper and thyme. Drizzle over the vinegar and oil. Marinate, turning occasionally, for up to 1 hour at room temperature or up to 4 hours in the refrigerator.

• Preheat a cast-iron ridged grill pan or barbecue. Grill the chops until medium rare, 3 minutes per side. Sprinkle with salt. Serve hot on warmed plates with lemon wedges and Sizzling Garlic Greens (see page 93).

Red Lentil **Dhal** with Aromatics

• For the dhal, melt the butter in a pan over a medium high heat. Add the onion, garlic and ginger and cook, stirring constantly, until fragrant, 1-2 minutes. Add the lentils, turmeric and water and bring to a boil. Turn down the heat and simmer, stirring occasionally, until thickened slightly, 20 - 30 minutes. Add salt to taste.

• For the aromatics, melt the butter in a small frying pan over medium high heat. Add the chilli flakes, bay, cumin, fennel and garlic and cook until the garlic is golden, 30-60 seconds. Stir into the dhal and serve immediately with steamed rice.

Moroccan Chicken Stew with Saffron and Apricot

SERVES 4
60g (2oz) butter
2 onions, finely chopped
4 garlic cloves, crushed
pinch saffron threads
1 tbsp turmeric
1½ tsp ground cumin
1½ tsp ground coriander
1½ tsp paprika
1 tsp black pepper
¼ tsp cayenne
8 chicken thighs, skinned
juice of 1 lemon
250ml (8floz) chicken stock
   or water
125g (4oz) dried apricots
400g (14oz) tin chickpeas,
   drained
salt

• Melt the butter in a heavy-based pan over medium low heat. Add the onions, garlic, saffron, turmeric, cumin, coriander, paprika, pepper and cayenne and cook, stirring occasionally, until onions are very soft, 10 minutes.
• Add the chicken, lemon juice, stock, apricots and chickpeas and bring just to simmering point. Cook gently until the chicken is tender and opaque throughout, with no trace of pink at the bone, 30-40 minutes. Add salt to taste.
•Arrange the chicken pieces on warmed plates and spoon over the sauce. Scatter with add-ons, if using. Serve hot, with buttered couscous or warm flatbread.

COOK'S TIP
The stew can be made up to 1 day in advance. Cover and refrigerate.

MOROCCAN CHICKEN STEW ADD-ONS
Add a final flourish of colour, texture and flavour to this sweetly spiced stew with 1 handful coriander or parsley or mint leaves and 2 tbsp flaked almonds.

VARIATION
Moroccan Lamb Stew with Saffron and Apricot
Replace chicken with 1kg (2lb) cubed stewing lamb, such as shoulder. Omit lemon juice and replace with the juice of 1 orange. Proceed as directed, but cover the pan tightly and cook very gently, taking care not to let the liquid boil. Cook until the lamb is very tender, 2-3 hours. Serve as directed.

SERVES 4
FOR THE LEMON MUSTARD
VINAIGRETTE
1 tsp dijon mustard
2 tbsp lemon juice
5 tbsp extra virgin olive oil
salt, black pepper

4 - 175g (6oz) fish
  fillets (see below)
1 tbsp extra virgin
  olive oil

WHY ORGANIC?
Organic farmed fish is given natural feeds only and is farmed in a way that minimalises harm to the environment. The fish can swim freely and do not undergo routine medication.

For healthy, ocean caught fish, buy from a supplier who sells fish caught from unpolluted waters, using sustainable fishing methods that do not deplete stocks. If your supplier doesn't, ask why not.

Grilled Fish with Lemon Mustard Vinaigrette

• Preheat an overhead grill to as hot as possible, allowing 15 minutes.
• For the dressing, combine mustard, lemon and oil in a small pan. Add salt and pepper to taste. Place over a low heat and warm through until tepid. 1-2 minutes.
• Place the fish skin-side up on an oiled oven tray. Grill, without turning, until cooked through (see below). Sprinkle with salt and pepper. Serve on warmed plates with the warmed dressing spooned over.

WHICH FISH?
Grill thin fish fillets about 1cm (½in) thick, such as sole, trout, grey mullet, red snapper, plaice or sea bass until just opaque throughout, 3-5 minutes.

Grill thick fish fillets about 2.5cm (1in) thick, such as cod, haddock, swordfish or turbot until just opaque throughout, 8-10 minutes.

Grill salmon fillets until the flesh turns opaque but is still moist and pink in the middle, 6-8 minutes.

VARIATIONS
Grilled Fish with Lemon Tomato Vinaigrette
Make vinaigrette as directed, adding 1 finely seeded and diced tomato.

Grilled Fish with Lemon Herb Vinaigrette
Make vinaigrette as directed, adding 1 tsp finely chopped fresh thyme, tarragon, parsley, fennel, dill or oregano.

Grilled Fish with Lemon Caper Vinaigrette
Make vinaigrette as directed, adding 1 tbsp drained and rinsed capers.

Wine-Glazed Steak with Mushrooms

SERVES 4

1 tbsp olive oil
2 garlic cloves, crushed
4 shallots, finely chopped
200g (7oz) wild mushrooms, chopped
4 - 250g (8oz) sirloin or rump steaks, 2.5cm (1in) thick
125ml (4floz) red wine
1 tsp butter
salt, black pepper

• Heat the oil in a heavy frying pan. Add the garlic, shallots and mushrooms and cook, stirring constantly, over high heat, until wilted and starting to crisp, 5 minutes. Remove from the pan and reserve.

• Add the steaks to the hot pan. Cook for 3 minutes per side for rare, 4 minutes per side for medium rare, 6 minutes per side for well done. Remove to warmed plates to rest.

• Add the wine to the hot pan. Boil until reduced by half, 2 minutes. Return the mushrooms to the pan. Heat through, stirring constantly, 1 minute. Remove from heat and stir in butter. Spoon mushrooms and wine juices over the steaks. Sprinkle with salt and pepper. Serve immediately.

VARIATION

Wine-Glazed Fillet Steak

Replace sirloin or rump steaks with 175g (6oz) fillet steaks, 5cm (2in) thick. Cook as directed, for 3 minutes per side for rare, 4 minutes per side for medium rare, 6 minutes per side for well done.

Eat Your Greens

Red Peppers stewed with Potatoes and Olives

SERVES 4 AS A MAIN, 6 AS A SIDE

4 tbsp extra virgin olive oil
1 onion, finely sliced
4 garlic cloves, finely sliced
¼ tsp crushed chilli flakes
3 red peppers, cored, seeded and cut into 5cm (2in) long and 2.5cm (1in) wide strips
4 medium potatoes, cut into 5cm (2in) chunks
400g (14oz) tin italian plum tomatoes, chopped
150g (5oz) pitted black olives
1 handful fresh basil or parsley, chopped
salt, black pepper

• Heat the oil in a heavy based pot. Add the onion and cook, stirring frequently, over medium heat until soft and just golden, 5 minutes.
• Add the garlic, chilli flakes, pepper, potato, tomatoes and olives. Turn the heat to low and simmer gently, stirring occasionally, until the potatoes are tender, 30-40 minutes. Stir in the basil or parsley. Add salt and pepper to taste. Serve hot or at room temperature.

Sizzling Garlic Greens

SERVES 4 AS A SIDE

2 tbsp extra virgin olive oil
2 garlic cloves, finely sliced
¼ tsp crushed chilli flakes
300g - 500g (10oz–1lb) greens (see opposite)
2 tsp red wine vinegar or lemon juice
salt, black pepper

• Heat the oil in a large frying pan. Add the garlic and chilli flakes and cook over medium high heat until the garlic is just golden, 1 minute.
• Add the greens and cook, stirring occasionally, until wilted and tender but still bright green (see below). Add the vinegar or lemon juice and salt and pepper to taste. Serve hot.

HEALTH BITE
Vitamin-rich and calcium-packed, dark leafy greens are super-charged with anti-carcinogenic antioxidants.

WHICH GREENS?
Any greens work for this recipe, but the cooking time will vary. Choose from:

500g (1lb) spinach or swiss chard, washed, stems finely chopped and leaves coarsely chopped. Cook for 5-8 minutes.
500g (1lb) cabbage, core cut out and discarded, leaves coarsely shredded. Cook for 15-20 minutes.
500g (1lb) green or purple sprouting broccoli, stems finely sliced, florets separated. Steam over boiling, salted water until the stems are just tender, 6-8 minutes. Add to garlic and chilli flakes in pan as directed. Cook for 5-7 minutes.
300g (10oz) kale, coarsely chopped. Cook for 15-20 minutes.
300g (10oz) spring greens, coarsely chopped. Cook for 15-20 minutes.

Smashed Potatoes

SERVES 4 AS A SIDE

1kg (2lb) potatoes, cut into
  equal-sized chunks
2 garlic cloves
175ml (6floz) milk, sour
  cream, double cream,
  crème fraîche or reserved
  potato cooking water
4 tbsp olive oil or 60g (2oz)
  butter
salt, black pepper, nutmeg

HEALTH BITE

Leaving the skin on the potatoes
adds extra nutrition and an earthy
flavour to smashed potatoes. It's up
to you how calorific you make your
smash. Your options range from
fat-free but nutritionally enhanced
potato water to richly indulgent
crème fraîche.

• Place the potato chunks and garlic in a pot of salted water to cover. Bring to the boil. Adjust the heat and simmer until soft, 20-30 minutes. Drain, reserving the potato water, if using.
• Return the potatoes to the dry pot. Return pot to a very low heat. Smash potatoes with a wooden spoon, beating in milk, sour cream, double cream, crème fraîche or cooking water. Beat in olive oil or butter. Add salt, pepper and nutmeg to taste. Serve immediately.

VARIATIONS

Horseradish Smashed Potatoes

Add 2 tbsp horseradish sauce to the smashed potatoes. Mix until combined.

Goat's Cheese Smashed Potatoes

Add 125g (4oz) crumbled goat's cheese to the smashed potatoes. Mix until combined.

Parsley Smashed Potatoes

Add 1 handful coarsely chopped parsley to the smashed potatoes. Mix until combined.

Mustard Smashed Potatoes

Add 2 tbsp creamy and 2 tbsp grainy dijon mustard to the smashed potatoes. Mix until combined.

Carrot Smashed Potatoes

Add 2 grated carrots to the smashed potatoes. Mix until combined.

Pesto Smashed Potatoes

Add 4 tbsp pesto to the smashed potatoes. Mix until combined.

Smashed Winter Roots

Replace half the potatoes with celeriac, parsnips, swede or turnips, or a combination, cut into equal-sized chunks. Cook as directed.

Roast Winter Squash

- Preheat oven to 200°C (400°F) Gas 6.
- Combine the garlic and oil. Cut the squash in half lengthwise and scoop out the seeds. Brush the flesh with the garlic oil. Sprinkle with salt and pepper. Place cut side down on a baking sheet.
- Roast until the skin is wrinkled and the flesh is very soft, about 1 hour. If necessary, cut into portions. Serve hot, cut side up, with salt, pepper and olive oil or butter. Alternatively, use to make Roast Winter Squash Mash (see below).

VARIATIONS

Roast Winter Squash Mash with Ginger

Roast the squash as directed. Scrape away the flesh from the skin and place in a food processor with 30g (1oz) butter and 1 tbsp grated fresh ginger; purée until smooth. Add salt and pepper to taste. Serve hot.

Roast Winter Squash Mash with Crème Fraîche and Cheese

Roast the squash as directed. Scrape away the flesh from the skin and place in a food processor with 30g (1oz) butter, 4 tbsp grated gruyère, parmesan or cheddar and 2 tbsp crème fraîche; purée until smooth. Add salt, pepper and nutmeg to taste. Serve hot.

SERVES 4 AS A SIDE
1 garlic clove, crushed
1 tbsp extra virgin olive oil
1.5kg (3lb) winter squash (about 1 large or 2 small squash)
salt, black pepper
olive oil or butter to serve

COOK'S TIP
Squashes differ in size and shape but they nearly all have bright orange or yellow flesh and a sweet, earthy flavour, both intensified by oven-roasting.
When roasted, winter squash makes a richly coloured and flavoured side dish for grilled or roast meats. For a vegetarian main meal, choose smaller squashes and serve one half per person, with plenty of butter, grated cheese and a scraping of nutmeg.

HEALTH BITE
Squash are chock-full of nutrients, low in calories, high in Vitamin A and potassium, and are one of the easiest vegetables to digest.

SERVES 4
500g (1lb) raw beetroot
175ml (6floz) double
  cream
125g (4oz) gruyère or
  cheddar cheese, grated
salt, black pepper

COOK'S TIP
Cut off the leaves from raw beetrot
when cooking, but do not peel or
trim root ends as this releases all
the colour into the water.
Alternatively, use pre-cooked
beetroot.

Creamy Beetroot
Gratin

- To cook beetroot, place whole in boiling water. Simmer until tender when pierced with the tip of a knife, 35-45 minutes, depending on size. Leave to cool. Peel and cut into 5mm (¼in) slices.
- Preheat oven to 200°C (400°F) Gas 6.
- Layer the beetroot slices in a buttered baking dish. Pour over the cream and sprinkle with cheese, salt and pepper.
- Bake until the topping is golden and just crisp, 15-20 minutes.

VARIATIONS

Creamy Parsnip Gratin

Omit beetroot and replace with 750g (1½ lb) medium parsnips, cut into 5mm (¼in) slices. Cook in boiling water until tender when pierced with the tip of a knife, 5-8 minutes. Drain well and proceed as directed.

Creamy Potato Gratin

Omit beetroot and replace with 750g (1½ lb) potatoes, cut into 5mm (¼in) slices. Cook in boiling water until tender when pierced with the tip of a knife, 5-8 minutes. Drain well and proceed as directed.

Creamy Turnip Gratin

Omit beetroot and replace with 750g (1½ lb) medium turnips, cut into 5mm (¼in) slices. Cook in boiling water until tender when pierced with the tip of a knife, 5-8 minutes. Drain well and proceed as directed.

Slow **Roast** Tomatoes

SERVES 4 AS A SIDE

6 ripe tomatoes, halved
2 garlic cloves
salt, black pepper
1 tbsp balsamic vinegar
2 tbsp extra virgin olive oil
additional extra virgin olive oil
  for serving
1 handful fresh herbs,
  chopped, such as parsley,
  basil, marjoram or a
  combination

COOK'S TIP

When cooking with fresh tomatoes
outside peak season, it is well
worth thinking ahead and buying
the tomatoes a few days in advance
of using. Set them on a tray,
making sure they are not touching,
by the kitchen window. Never
store tomatoes in the refrigerator,
as refrigeration spoils their texture
and aroma.

- Preheat the oven to 120°C (250°F) Gas ½.
- Place the tomatoes on an oven tray, cut side up. Cut garlic clove in half and cut each half into 3 slivers. Lay a sliver of garlic onto each tomato half. Sprinkle each tomato half with a pinch of salt and pepper. Drizzle over the vinegar and oil. Slow roast until very soft and wilted, 2 hours.
- Serve hot or at room temperature, drizzled with additional olive oil and scattered with fresh herbs.

Marinated Beans with Olive Oil, Lemon and Chilli

• For the dressing, combine the garlic, lemon juice, oil and chilli flakes. Add salt and pepper to taste.

• Place the beans in a pan of water to cover. Bring just to the boil. Drain immediately and combine the hot beans with the dressing. Toss gently to coat. Add the tomatoes and the herbs. Add salt and pepper to taste. Serve while still warm with grilled meats or fish, or at room temperature with green salad leaves.

WHICH BEANS?

white haricot, cannellini, flageolet, borlotti beans or chickpeas all work well with this recipe.

SERVES 4

2 garlic cloves, crushed
2 tbsp lemon juice
5 tbsp extra virgin olive oil
¼ tsp crushed chilli flakes
salt, black pepper
2 - 400g (14oz) tins beans (see below), drained and rinsed
4 ripe tomatoes, diced
1 handful fresh parsley or basil, coarsely chopped

COOK'S TIP

If you are using dried beans, you will need 250g (8oz). Soak overnight in water to cover. Drain, rinse and cook in water to cover until tender, 1-1½ hours. Be sure to combine with the dressing while still hot.

HEALTH BITE

Dried beans and pulses are now recognised as one of nature's healthiest foods - low in fat, high in fibre, rich in iron, phosphorous and B vitamins. As well as being a good source of protein, their high carbohydrate content delivers a gradual release of energy.

Roast Winter Roots

SERVES 4 AS A SIDE

1.25kg (2½ lb) mixed root vegetables (see opposite)

1 head garlic, separated into cloves but unpeeled

½ tsp crumbled dried rosemary or 1 tsp finely chopped fresh rosemary

½ tbsp balsamic vinegar

4 tbsp extra virgin olive oil

coarse salt, black pepper

HEALTH BITE

Leave skins on root vegetables where possible, as the skin and the flesh just beneath the skin are valuable nutritionally, containing the most fibre and vitamin C.

- Preheat the oven to 200°C (400°F) Gas 6.
- Place the vegetables and garlic in a single layer in a roasting dish. Sprinkle with rosemary, vinegar, oil, salt and pepper. Toss well to coat. Roast until golden and tender, 40 minutes - 1 hour.

WHICH ROOTS?

Any roots or combination of roots will work for this recipe. To minimize differences in cooking times, you will need to cut the fast-cooking vegetables into slightly larger pieces than the slow-cookers. Choose from:

potatoes, quartered
carrots, halved lengthwise
medium parsnips, quartered lengthwise
celeriac, peeled and cut into wedges
turnips, quartered
sweet potatoes, quartered
beetroot, quartered
shallots, whole and peeled
onions, peeled and quartered but still attached by the root end
swede, peeled and cut into wedges
jerusalem artichokes, halved

Spring Vegetable Ragoût

SERVES 4 AS A MAIN, 6 AS A SIDE

2 tbsp extra virgin olive oil
750g (1½ lb) mixed spring
  vegetables (see opposite)
lemon wedges
150ml (5floz) boiling
  vegetable stock or water
2 tsp butter
2 tbsp lemon juice
salt, black pepper
1 handful fresh herbs, torn
  or roughly chopped
  (see opposite)

• Heat the oil in a large frying pan. Add the vegetables and cook, stirring constantly, over medium heat until just starting to soften, 5 minutes. Add the boiling stock or water and simmer until the vegetables are crisp-tender, 10 minutes.

• Remove from heat and add butter and lemon juice. Add salt and pepper to taste. Ladle into warmed bowls, scatter with fresh herbs and serve hot.

WHICH VEGETABLES?

Any combination of tender spring vegetables will work for this recipe. To minimize differences in cooking times, you need to cut the fast-cooking vegetables into slightly larger pieces than the slow-cookers. Choose from:

asparagus, cut into 7.5cm (3in) lengths
radishes, halved
button mushrooms, whole
spring onions, cut into 7.5cm (3in) lengths
cherry tomatoes, whole
carrots, cut into sticks 7.5cm x 1cm (3in x ½in)
broad beans, shelled
peas, shelled
fennel, halved and sliced 1cm (½in) thick
snow peas, whole
zucchini, cut into sticks 1cm (½in) thick and 7.5cm (2in) long
green beans, whole
spring turnips, cut into 7.5cm x 1cm (3in x ½in) sticks
celery sticks, cut into 7.5cm x 1cm (3in x ½in) sticks
cauliflower cut into tiny florets
purple sprouting or green broccoli, leaves and stalks chopped and heads cut into tiny florets

WHICH HERBS?

Try any one or a combination of fresh herbs. Our preference is for the classic *fines herbes* quartet - chervil, chives, parsley and tarragon.

Best Baked Potatoes

• Arrange the oven rack in the centre of the oven. Place a baking sheet on the rack. Preheat the oven to 200°C (400°F) Gas 6.
• Pierce the potatoes a few times with a fork or skewer. Rinse the potatoes under cold running water. While they are still damp, sprinkle evenly with salt. Place the potatoes at least 10 cm (4in) apart on to the hot baking sheet. Bake until crusty outside and soft inside, 1-1½ hours.
• To serve, cut a cross on the top of each potato. Push the ends together to open it up. Sprinkle with salt and pepper. Add butter or oil. Serve hot, as a side with roasts or stews, or make a meal of it served with a salad.

VARIATION
Best Baked Potato with Cherry Tomatoes
This is our favourite topping. Make the Roast Cherry Tomatoes on page 68. Cook and cut open the potatoes as directed. Top with greek-style yoghurt or sour cream, then spoon over the tomatoes.

BEST BAKED POTATO GO-WITHS
Finish with any one or a combination of the following:
125ml (4floz) sour cream or greek-style yoghurt
125g (4oz) grated cheese
2 tbsp finely chopped chives or spring onions

Best Baked Sweet Potato

• Arrange the oven rack in the centre of the oven. Preheat the oven to 200°C (400°F) Gas 6.
• Pierce the potatoes a few times with a fork or skewer. Place the potatoes at least 10cm (4in) apart in an oven tray. Bake until very soft, 1-1½ hours.
• To serve, cut a cross on the top of each potato. Push the ends together to open it up. Sprinkle with salt, pepper, nutmeg and cinnamon. Serve hot with butter.

SERVES 4
4 – (250g) 8oz potatoes
salt, black pepper

TO SERVE
1 large knob of butter or
 1 tbsp olive oil per potato

COOK'S TIP
Never bake potatoes either in the microwave or in the oven wrapped in foil, or the potatoes will be steamed, not baked.

SERVES 4
4 sweet potatoes
salt, pepper, nutmeg,
 cinnamon

TO SERVE
1 large knob of butter
 per potato

COOK'S TIP
We recommend using an oven tray with sides, rather than a baking sheet, because sweet potatoes tend to leak syrupy juices as they bake.

Dressings for Leafy Salads

Honey Mustard

**EACH MAKES ENOUGH TO DRESS
4 HANDFULS SALAD LEAVES**
1 garlic clove, crushed
1 tbsp honey
1 tsp creamy dijon mustard
2 tsp grainy dijon mustard
2 tbsp red wine vinegar
5 tbsp extra virgin olive oil
salt, black pepper

• Mix together garlic, honey, mustards, vinegar and olive oil until thick and smooth. Add salt and pepper to taste.

Lemon Garlic

SERVES 4
1 garlic clove, crushed
2 tbsp lemon juice
5 tbsp extra virgin olive oil
salt, black pepper

• Mix together garlic, lemon and oil until smooth. Add salt and pepper to taste.

Avocado Yoghurt

SERVES 4
1 avocado
1 garlic clove, crushed
2 spring onions, chopped
125g (4oz) greek-style
  yoghurt
1 tbsp red wine vinegar
1 tbsp extra virgin olive oil
salt, black pepper

• Place avocado, garlic, spring onion, yoghurt, vinegar and oil in a food processor; pulse until smooth. Add salt and pepper to taste.

Creamy Shallot

SERVES 4
1 shallot, finely chopped
2 tbsp red wine vinegar
4 tbsp extra virgin olive oil
4 tbsp crème fraîche or sour
  cream
salt, black pepper

• Mix together the shallot, vinegar, oil and crème fraîche or sour cream until thick and smooth. Add salt and pepper to taste.

COOK'S TIP
You can make any of these dressings up to 1 day in advance. Cover and refrigerate. For the avocado dressing, be sure to press cling film directly on the surface to keep from it turning brown.

Balsamic Baked Onions

SERVES 4

4 medium to large onions,
  red or yellow, peeled with
  root ends intact
2 tbsp extra virgin olive oil
2 tbsp balsamic vinegar
salt, black pepper

HEALTH BITE
Onions, like their relative garlic,
are a good source of heart-
protective antioxidants.

• Preheat the oven to 200°C (400°F) Gas 6.
• Cut a deep cross about 5cm (2in) deep in the top of each onion. Place the onions in a baking dish with a few tablespoons of water. Drizzle over oil and vinegar. Sprinkle with salt and pepper. Cover with foil and bake for 30 minutes. Remove the foil and bake until very tender and lightly crisp around the edges, 30 minutes.
• Spread the onions open. Serve hot, with add-ons (see below), if using.

BALSAMIC BAKED ONIONS ADD-ONS
Sprinkle over any or a combination of the following ingredients to transform these slow-cooked onions from side dish to main event:

125g (4oz) crumbled blue cheese
125ml (4floz) sour cream
125g (4oz) grated cheddar or gruyère cheese

New Potato Salad with Shallot Vinaigrette

SERVES 4 AS A SIDE
750g (1½ lb) new potatoes,
   cut into bite-size pieces
2 shallots, finely chopped, or
   4 spring onions finely sliced
2 tbsp red wine vinegar
4 tbsp extra virgin olive oil
salt, black pepper

• Place the potato pieces in a large pan of cold water. Bring to a boil. Adjust heat and simmer gently until tender but still firm when pierced with the tip of a knife, 10-15 minutes. Drain.

• While the potatoes are cooking, make the vinaigrette. Mix shallots, vinegar and oil until combined.

• Add the hot potatoes to the vinaigrette with mix-ins, if using. Toss gently to coat each potato piece. Add salt and pepper to taste. Serve warm or at room temperature.

COOK'S TIP
If serving the salad warm, you can cook and dress the potatoes up to 45 minutes in advance. If serving at room temperature, you can make the salad up to 1 day in advance. Cover and refrigerate, but, for optimum flavour, be sure to return to room temperature before serving.

VARIATION
New Potato Salad with Crème Fraîche

Prepare the potatoes and vinaigrette as directed. Add 125ml (4floz) crème fraîche and mix gently to coat evenly.

NEW POTATO SALAD MIX-INS
Vary the flavour and texture of this classic French-style potato salad by adding 2 tbsp finely chopped fresh herbs, such as dill, parsley or chives, 1 tbsp grainy dijon mustard or 2 celery stalks, finely chopped.

Something Sweet

Upside Down Red Plum
Caramel Cake

SERVES 6-8

FOR THE CARAMEL
175g (6oz) sugar
6 tbsp water
4 large red plums, halved

FOR THE CAKE
150g (5oz) flour
2 tsp baking powder
175g (6oz) butter, softened
175g (6oz) granulated sugar
4 tbsp ground almonds
4 eggs, beaten
1 tsp vanilla extract

ESSENTIAL EQUIPMENT
25cm (10in) cake tin, buttered

COOK'S TIP
Caramel is basically burnt sugar. There are just a few important points to remember in order to guarantee caramel success every time. Once the syrup has boiled, do not stir as this encourages crystallization. If your caramel is colouring too fast, prevent further cooking by plunging the base of the pan into cold water. If it sets too hard to pour, return the pan to a low heat and warm gently until it melts.

• Preheat the oven to 150°C (300°F) Gas 2. Butter the cake tin.
• Place the sugar and water in a heavy-based pan over a low heat. Stir constantly with a wooden spoon to dissolve sugar. Do not allow the liquid to boil until the sugar has completely dissolved to form a clear syrup. Raise the heat to medium and bring the syrup to a boil. Boil rapidly until the syrup starts to turn brown around the edge of the pan. Lower the heat and continue to cook to a dark golden brown. Do not stir with a spoon, but swirl the pan once or twice so that the caramel colours evenly. Pour immediately into the buttered tin.
• Arrange the plums skin side up over the caramel.
• Sift the flour and baking powder into a large bowl. Add butter, sugar, almonds, eggs and vanilla. Beat until just smooth and evenly blended, 1-2 minutes. Spread the cake mixture over the fruit. Bake until the top is golden brown and the sides of the cake have pulled away from the tin, about 50 minutes.
• Leave to cool for 2-3 minutes, then run a knife around the sides of the cake and turn out onto a serving dish. If any pieces of fruit stick to the tin, use a spatula to remove and press back into place. Serve warm or at room temperature.

VARIATIONS

Upside Down Strawberry Caramel Cake
Replace plums with 1kg (2lb) ripe strawberries. Proceed as directed.

Upside Down Mango Caramel Cake
Replace plums with 3 medium, sliced mangoes. Proceed as directed.

Upside Down Apple Caramel Cake
Replace plums with 4 quartered apples. Proceed as directed.

Quick-Fix Toppings for Vanilla Ice-Cream

Toffee Bananas

SERVES 4

5 tbsp soft brown sugar
60g (2oz) butter
6 tbsp double cream
vanilla ice cream
2 bananas, diagonally sliced

• Place the sugar, butter and cream in a small pan over medium heat and bring to the boil, stirring constantly.
• Have the ice-cream ready in bowls. Top with banana slices. Drizzle over hot toffee sauce. Serve immediately.

Very Berry

SERVES 4

250g (8oz) blueberries,
   blackberries, raspberries,
   strawberries or
   a combination
2 tbsp sugar
vanilla ice cream

• Place the berries and sugar in a heavy pan over a low heat. Cook, stirring occasionally, until it is hot through and the juices start to run, about 10 minutes. Do not allow to boil.
• Have the ice-cream ready in bowls. Spoon over hot berries and juices. Serve immediately.

Chocolate Fudge

SERVES 4

125ml (4floz) double cream
1 tbsp dark brown sugar
15g (1oz) butter
125g (4oz) dark chocolate,
   broken into pieces
1 tsp vanilla extract
vanilla ice cream

• Heat the cream, sugar and butter in a small pan until just simmering. Remove from the heat. Add the chocolate and vanilla and leave to stand for 1 minute. Stir until smooth and glossy.
• Have the ice-cream ready in bowls. Drizzle over the hot sauce. Serve immediately.

Caramelized Apples

SERVES 4

60g (2oz) butter
4 tbsp light brown sugar
4 ripe firm apples, cored and
   cut into 8 pieces
4 tbsp water
vanilla ice cream

• Melt the butter in a large frying pan over medium heat. Add the sugar and stir to dissolve. Add the apples and cook, shaking the pan frequently, until the apples are golden brown, 5 minutes. Add the water and simmer until the apples are tender, 2 minutes.
• Have the ice-cream ready in bowls. Top with hot apples and juices. Serve immediately.

Peach-Ginger **Crisp** with Oatmeal

- Preheat the oven to 190°C (375°F) Gas 5.
- Place the peaches, sugar, lemon and ginger in a 20cm x 26cm x 5cm (8in x 10in x 2in) buttered baking dish and toss together gently to combine.
- For the topping, place the flour, oatmeal, salt, sugar and butter in a food processor; pulse until coarse and crumbly. Alternatively, mix the flour, oatmeal, salt and sugar in a bowl. Use 2 knives to cut the butter into the flour mixture until coarse and crumbly.
- Cover the fruit with the topping and bake until the topping is golden brown and the fruit is tender, 45 minutes. Serve hot.

VARIATIONS

Apple-Cinnamon Crisp with Oatmeal

Replace peaches with 6 cored and sliced apples. Replace ginger with 1 tsp cinnamon. Proceed as directed.

Strawberry-Rhubarb Crisp with Oatmeal

Replace peaches with 1kg (2lb) rhubarb cut into 1cm (½in) pieces and 250g (8oz) halved strawberries. Omit ginger and increase sugar to 175g (6oz). Proceed as directed.

Nectarine-Raspberry Crisp with Oatmeal

Replace peaches with 4 nectarines sliced 1cm (½in) thick and 250g (8oz) raspberries. Omit ginger. Proceed as directed.

Blueberry-Pear Crisp with Oatmeal

Replace peaches with 4 cored and sliced pears and 250g (8oz) blueberries. Omit ginger. Proceed as directed.

SERVES 4-6

6 peaches, sliced 1cm (½ in) thick
2 tbsp sugar
1 tbsp lemon juice
2 tbsp grated fresh ginger

FOR THE TOPPING
100g (3½ oz) plain flour
60g (2oz) oatmeal
¼ tsp salt
175g (6oz) light brown sugar
125g (4oz) butter, chilled and cubed

HEALTH BITE
Oats are an excellent source of iron, magnesium and soluable fibre, and are low in saturated fat and sodium. Eaten regularly, oats may also help to lower cholesterol levels.

Easy Vanilla Fudge Brownies

MAKES 12

300g (10oz) dark chocolate
175g (6oz) butter
150g (5oz) sugar
2 tsp vanilla extract
4 eggs, beaten
125g (4oz) plain flour
2 tbsp cocoa powder
75g (2½ oz) chopped walnuts
  or pecan nuts
vanilla ice cream to serve

ESSENTIAL EQUIPMENT
34cm x 24cm x 5cm (13in x 9in x 2in) baking tin

• Line the baking tray with foil, letting it come up above the sides of the tray by about 5cm (2in).
• Preheat the oven to 150°C (300°F) Gas 2.
• Place the chocolate and butter in a heavy pan over a low heat. Stir constantly until smooth and glossy. Remove from the heat and leave to cool until tepid. Whisk the sugar, vanilla and eggs into the chocolate mixture until well blended. Stir in the flour, cocoa and walnuts or pecans until just combined.
• Pour into the lined tray and bake until the top is firm to the touch but the interior is still slightly gooey, 45 minutes. Place on a wire rack to cool completely. Use the foil to lift the brownie out of the tin. Cut into squares and carefully peel off the foil. Serve with a scoop of vanilla ice cream.

Luscious Lemon Cheesecake

• Preheat the oven to 180°C (350°F) Gas 4.

• Combine the almonds, sugar, salt and butter. Press evenly on to the base of the tin. Bake until crisp, 10 minutes. Cool on a wire rack.

• Place the cream cheese in a bowl with the sugar, lemon zest and juice and beat briefly until smooth and creamy. Beat in the eggs a quarter at a time until just incorporated, scraping down the sides of the bowl after each addition.

• Spread the cheesecake mixture over the crust. Set the tin on a baking sheet and bake until the centre wobbles slightly when the tin is tapped, about 45 minutes.

• For the topping, combine the sour cream, sugar and lemon juice. Spread over the baked cheesecake. Return to the oven and bake for another 5 minutes. Cool completely in the tin on a wire rack. Cover and chill in the refrigerator for at least 3 hours, preferably overnight.

• To unmould, run a knife around the sides of the cheesecake. Release the springform clip and remove the sides of the tin. Serve chilled, cut into slices.

VARIATIONS

Luscious Lime Cheesecake

Omit lemon zest and juice and replace with the grated zest of 1½ limes and 2 tbsp lime juice for the filling, and 1 tbsp lime juice for the topping. Proceed as directed.

Luscious Grapefruit Cheesecake

Omit lemon zest and juice and replace with the grated zest of ½ yellow grapefruit and 2 tbsp yellow grapefruit juice for the filling, and 1 tbsp yellow grapefruit juice for the topping. Proceed as directed.

SERVES 6-8

FOR THE CRUST
200g (7oz) ground almonds
3 tbsp sugar
pinch salt
4 tbsp melted butter

FOR THE FILLING
1kg (2lb) cream cheese
350g (12oz) granulated sugar
grated zest of 1 lemon
2 tbsp lemon juice
4 eggs, beaten

FOR THE TOPPING
250ml (8floz) sour cream
4 tbsp sugar
1 tbsp lemon juice

ESSENTIAL EQUIPMENT
1 - 25cm (10in) springform cake tin

HEALTH BITE
Lemon peel contains more vitamin C than the flesh itself, but non-organic lemons are treated with waxes, fungicides and post-harvest sprays to prolong shelf-life and improve eye-appeal. These cannot be completely removed by washing. If you can't find organic lemons to zest, we advise leaving out the grated zest altogether.

SERVES 6-8
FOR THE CAKE
150g (5oz) butter
400g (14oz) dark chocolate,
  broken into pieces
150g (5oz) granulated sugar
5 eggs, separated

FOR THE GLAZE
175ml (6floz) double cream
175g (6oz) dark chocolate,
  broken into pieces

ESSENTIAL EQUIPMENT
1 - 25cm (10in) cake tin, but-
tered and lined with baking
parchment

COOK'S TIP
How do you tell when you have
whisked the egg whites to soft
peaks? Lift up some of the egg
white foam with the whisk – the
peaks will hold their shape but
droop slightly when the whisk is
lifted out.

Chocolate **Truffle** Torte

• Preheat the oven to 150°C (300°F) Gas 2. Butter and line the cake tin.
• For the cake, place the butter and chocolate in a heavy pan over a low heat.
Stir constantly until smooth and glossy. Remove from the heat and leave to cool
until tepid. Whisk the sugar and egg yolks into the chocolate mixture.
• Place the egg whites in a large bowl and whisk until soft peaks form. Use a
rubber spatula to fold a quarter of the egg whites gently into the chocolate
mixture. Add this mixture to the remaining egg whites and gently fold together.
Pour into the prepared tin. Bake until the top is firm to the touch but the
interior is still slightly gooey, 45 minutes. Leave to cool completely on a
wire rack.
• For the glaze, heat the cream in a small pan until just below simmering.
Remove from the heat. Add the chocolate and leave to stand for 1 minute. Stir
until smooth and glossy. Leave to cool until slightly thickened, 30 minutes.
• To unmould the cake, run a knife around the sides of the tin. Turn out and
peel off the paper. Reinvert onto a serving dish. Spread the glaze over the cake.
Serve in wedges, with garnishes if using.

CHOCOLATE TRUFFLE TORTE GARNISHES
You can serve this torte unadorned or dress it up with various simple garnishes.
Choose from:

strawberries, halved, or raspberries to decorate, cream, whipped,
thick or pouring, to serve, cocoa, to dust.

Or for an impressive final flourish, serve with a berry coulis. Liquidize a
handful of fresh or frozen strawberries and/or raspberries until
smooth. Drizzle this berry coulis around the wedges of torte just before
serving.

Spiced Apple Crumble Cake

- Preheat the oven to 190°C (375°F) Gas 5.
- For the crumble, place the flour, sugar and butter in a food processor; pulse until coarse and crumbly. Alternatively, mix the flour and sugar by hand and, using 2 knives, cut the butter into the flour mixture. Set aside.
- For the fruit, combine the apple slices with the sugar and cinnamon until evenly coated.
- For the cake, sift the flour and baking powder together and set aside. Beat the eggs together with the milk. In a large bowl, beat the butter until light and creamy. Gradually beat the sugar into the butter until white and fluffy. Gradually add the egg mixture, about 1 tbsp at a time, beating thoroughly after each addition. Use a rubber spatula to fold in the flour in 3 batches.
- Spread the cake mixture evenly into the prepared tin. Cover the cake mixture with the apples. Sprinkle the crumble over the apples. Bake until the crumble is golden brown, the apples are tender and the sides of the cake have pulled away from the tin, about 1 hour.
- Leave to cool on a wire rack for 15 minutes, then run a knife around the sides of the cake and turn out on to a serving dish. Serve warm or at room temperature.

VARIATIONS

Rhubarb and Ginger Crumble Cake

Replace apples with 750g (1½lb) rhubarb cut into 1cm (½in) pieces. Replace cinnamon with ground ginger. Proceed as directed.

Blackberry and Apple Crumble Cake

Reduce apples to 2 and add 250g (8oz) blackberries. Proceed as directed.

Cranberry and Orange Crumble Cake

Replace apples with 250g (8oz) cranberries. Add the grated zest of 1 orange. Increase the sugar to 4 tbsp. Proceed as directed.

SERVES 6-8

FOR THE CRUMBLE
125g (4oz) plain flour
60g (2oz) granulated sugar
90g (3oz) butter

FOR THE FRUIT
4 apples, sliced
1 tbsp sugar
1 tsp cinnamon

FOR THE CAKE
175g (6oz) plain flour
2 tsp baking powder
3 eggs
1 tbsp milk
175g (6oz) butter, softened
175g (6oz) granulated sugar

ESSENTIAL EQUIPMENT
1 - 25cm (10in) cake tin, buttered and lined with baking parchment

COOK'S TIP
The secret to successful cake-making is to have all the ingredients at room temperature. Here are 2 quick-fixes if you have forgotten to take the butter or eggs out of the refrigerator.
To soften butter, cut into small cubes. Place in a bowl set over another bowl of just boiled water, making sure the base of the bowl is not actually touching the water or the butter will melt, not soften. Set aside to soften, about 10 minutes.
To bring eggs to room temperature, place whole eggs in their shells in a bowl of hand-hot water for 10 minutes.

SERVES 8

FOR THE MERINGUE

6 egg whites
350g (12oz) caster sugar
2 tsp cornflour
1 tsp vinegar

FOR THE TOPPING

250ml (8floz) double cream
500g (1lb) strawberries,
  raspberries, blueberries or
  blackberries or a
  combination

COOK'S TIP

It is crucial that the bowl in which
you beat the egg whites is
completely grease-free or the egg
whites will not stiffen. If in doubt,
wipe with kitchen paper, dipping in
vinegar before you begin. To
achieve maximum volume, be sure
that the egg whites are at room
temperature before you beat them.
A daring but effective way to
check if the egg whites are
sufficiently stiff is to hold the bowl
upside down: the meringue should
not fall out.

Mini Pavlovas with Summer Berries

- Preheat the oven to 180°C (350°F) Gas 4.
- Line 2 baking sheets with baking parchment. Draw 4 – 10cm (4in) circles onto each parchment sheet.
- Place the egg whites in a large bowl and whisk until soft peaks form. Gradually whisk in the sugar, 1 tbsp at a time, whisking well after each addition. Whisk until the whites hold stiff peaks. Whisk in the cornflour and vinegar.
- Divide the meringue mixture equally among the circles. Spread into rounds with a rubber spatula. Use the back of a spoon to hollow out a nest. Bake for 5 minutes. Turn down the oven to 120°C (250°F) Gas ½. Bake until crisp on the outside and gooey inside, 45 minutes. Place on a wire rack to cool completely before peeling off the parchment paper.
- Whip the cream until just stiff. Top the pavlovas with cream. Arrange the berries over the cream. Serve chilled or at room temperature.

VARIATION
Mini Pavlovas with Banana and Chocolate

Omit summer berries and replace with 2 bananas, sliced and gently tossed in 2 tbsp lemon juice. Place 75g (2½oz) dark chocolate and 3 tbsp double cream in a small pan over a very low heat. Stir constantly until the chocolate has just melted. Remove from heat and stir until smooth and glossy. Leave to cool until slightly thickened, 5 minutes. Arrange bananas over cream. Drizzle over melted chocolate. Dust with cocoa powder to garnish.

Breakfast Anytime

Blue Moon
Muesli Smoothie

Place the blueberries, dates, oats, almonds, banana, apple juice and soy milk in a blender; whizz until smooth.

Banana Bliss
Smoothie

Place banana, soy milk, yoghurt and honey in a blender; whizz until smooth.

SERVES 1
4 tbsp blueberries
2 dried stoned dates
2 tbsp rolled oats
5 almonds
1 small banana
125ml (4floz) fresh apple juice
75ml (2½ floz) vanilla soy milk

SERVES 1
2 bananas
175ml (6floz) vanilla soy milk
4 tbsp yoghurt
1 tsp honey

HEALTH BITE
Potassium-rich and high in complex carbohydrates, bananas pack an energy-giving nutritional punch that makes them a great way to start the day.

Easily digestible, soy milk is a great substitute for those wishing or needing to avoid dairy milks. Low calorie, low in cholesterol and low in carbohydrate, it is also an excellent source of vegetable protein. Choosing organic soy milk is imperative if you wish to avoid GM soy products.

Berry Breakfast Pancakes

SERVES 4

300g (10oz) plain flour
1 tbsp baking powder
½ tsp salt
2 eggs, beaten
1 tbsp sugar
500ml (16floz) milk
2 tbsp melted butter
8 tbsp blueberries or
  raspberries or a combination
oil to brush griddle or pan

FOR SERVING
maple syrup or runny honey

ESSENTIAL EQUIPMENT

cast-iron griddle or large frying pan

- Preheat the oven to 180°C (350°F) Gas 4.
- Place the flour, baking powder and salt in a large bowl and make a well in the centre. Add the eggs, sugar, milk and butter to the well. Gradually draw in flour from the sides and whisk to a smooth batter. Gently stir in the berries. Transfer the batter to a measuring jug.
- Heat the griddle or pan over medium heat and brush with oil. Working in batches, pour enough batter to make 10cm (4in) pancakes onto the hot griddle or pan. Cook until bubbles appear on the surface and the underside is golden brown, 3 minutes. Turn pancake, pressing gently to ensure that the pancake is in contact with the griddle or pan. Cook until underside is brown, 2 minutes.
- Transfer the pancakes to a baking sheet and loosely cover with foil and keep warm in the oven while you cook the remaining pancakes. Brush the griddle or pan with oil between each batch of pancakes. Serve hot with maple syrup or runny honey.

VARIATIONS

Rice Breakfast Pancakes
Omit berries. Add 8 tbsp cooked brown or white rice to the batter. Proceed as directed.

Raisin Breakfast Pancakes
Omit berries. Add 8 tbsp raisins to the batter. Proceed as directed.

Wholewheat Breakfast Pancakes
Omit berries. Replace plain flour with wholemeal flour. Proceed as directed.

Yoghurt Breakfast Pancakes
Omit berries. Reduce milk to 250ml (8floz). Add 250ml (8floz) yoghurt with the eggs, sugar, milk and butter to the flour. Proceed as directed.

Banana Breakfast Pancakes
Omit berries. Have ready 1 sliced banana. Make batter as described. Pour batter on the hot griddle or pan and immediately place 2 slices of banana on top of each pancake. Proceed as directed.

New Orleans
French Toast

- Preheat the oven to 180°C (350°F) Gas 4.
- Place the eggs, sugar, salt, vanilla, cream and milk in a large bowl. Whisk until well blended and foaming. Dip the bread slices in the egg mixture, turning until well coated.
- Melt half the butter in a large non-stick frying pan over medium heat. Add half the dipped bread and cook until the underside is golden brown, 3 minutes. Turn and brown the other side, 2 minutes.
- Transfer to a baking sheet and keep warm in the oven while you cook the remaining bread. Add the remaining butter to the pan as needed. Serve hot with maple syrup or runny honey.

SERVES 4

3 eggs, beaten
1 tbsp sugar
¼ tsp salt
1 tsp vanilla extract
125ml (4floz) double cream
125ml (4floz) milk
8 slices day old white bread
125g (4oz) butter

FOR SERVING
maple syrup or runny honey

Mustard
Scrambled Eggs

- Melt the butter in a pan over medium low heat. Add the eggs and cook, stirring constantly, until just thickened. Add the cheese and stir until melted. Remove from the heat. Stir in the mustard, herbs and salt and pepper to taste. Serve immediately.

WHICH HERBS?
Vary the fresh herb according to what is available. Our preference would be any one or a combination of parsley, chives, spring onions, tarragon, watercress, sorrel or chervil.

SERVES 4

75g (2½ oz) butter
8 eggs, beaten
6 tbsp grated gruyère or
   cheddar cheese
2 tsp creamy dijon mustard
1 tbsp finely chopped fresh
   herbs (see opposite)
 salt, black pepper

Best Blueberry Yoghurt Muffins

MAKES 12

300g (10oz) plain flour
1 tbsp baking powder
½ tsp bicarbonate of soda
½ tsp salt
2 eggs, beaten
175g (6oz) light brown sugar
250ml (8floz) yoghurt
125ml (4oz) butter, melted
1 tsp vanilla extract
175g (6oz) blueberries
sugar and cinnamon
  for dusting

ESSENTIAL EQUIPMENT

*12-cup muffin tin, buttered or
lined with paper cups*

COOK'S TIP

You can bake muffins up to 1 day
in advance. Store in a sealed plastic
bag at room temperature.

• Preheat the oven to 190°C (375°F) Gas 5.
• Sift the flour, baking powder, bicarbonate of soda and salt into a large bowl.
Place the eggs, sugar, yoghurt, butter and vanilla in a second bowl and beat
until blended. Add the egg mixture to the flour with the blueberries. Use a
rubber spatula to fold together gently until just combined. Do not overmix; the
mixture should not be smooth. Divide the mixture among the muffin cups.
Sprinkle over a dusting of sugar and cinnamon.
• Bake until the edges shrink from the sides of the tin and a toothpick inserted
into the muffins comes out clean, 12-15 minutes.
• Leave the muffins in the tin for 5 minutes before removing. Run a knife
around the edges of the muffins. Turn out onto a wire rack. Serve while still
warm or at room temperature.

VARIATIONS

Spiced Banana Yoghurt Muffins

Replace the blueberries with 2 diced bananas and 2 tsp cinnamon. Proceed
as directed.

Cranberry Nut Yoghurt muffins

Replace the blueberries with 175g (6oz) cranberries and 60g (2oz) chopped
pecans or walnuts. Proceed as directed.

Lemon Pear Yoghurt Muffins

Replace blueberries with 2 diced pears and the grated zest of 1 lemon. Proceed
as directed.

Seasonal Menus

A Perfect Day for a Picnic

Good food always tastes better outdoors, whether on the beach, in the park, or at home on the lawn. Picnics call for dishes that travel well and this menu is perfectly portable. Everything can be made in advance. To ensure a crisp crust, let the pizzas cool completely on a wire rack before slicing and wrapping.

Spinach, Blue Cheese and Pine Nut Pizza (see page 49)
Marinated Beans with Lemon, Oil and Chilli (see page 101)
Roast Pepper, Artichoke and Feta Salad with Rocket (see page 42)

•

baguette or ciabatta
assorted cheeses

•

ripe melon slices and bunches of green grapes
Easy Vanilla Fudge Brownies (see page 120)

•

lemonade or limeade

An Autumn Harvest Menu

A richly coloured vegetarian menu that celebrates the turning of the season, when late summer produce is still gloriously abundant and the first winter squashes make their appearance on the market stalls.

Olive Oil Bruschetta with Red Pepper and Almond Pesto (see page 54)

•

Ginger Squash Soup (see page 30)

•

Mushroom Tart (see page 65)
Balsamic Baked Onions (see page 110)
Slow-Roast Tomatoes (see page 100)

•

Upside Down Red Plum Caramel Cake (see page 114)
crème fraîche

Sunny Sunday Wake-up Late Breakfast

Set the table in the garden, on the terrace or by an open window. Then relax and read the papers in the morning sunshine.

Blue Moon Muesli Smoothie (see page 133)

•

Mustard Scrambled Eggs (see page 137)

•

summer fruit bowl of peaches, cherries and apricots

•

coffee, tea

Self-Serve Dinner in a Bowl Party

Gently bubbling pots of soups on the stove make cooking for a crowd easy. Your guests are greeted by the comforting aromas of steaming soup and warm bread. If you like to bake, turn to page 53 for our focaccia recipe and choose from simple olive oil, rosemary, olive and onion, or, better still, serve a selection.

Tuscan Vegetable Soup with Greens and Beans (see page 20)
Carrot and Parsnip Soup with Ginger (see page 24)
Potato, Garlic and Fennel Soup (see page 23)
baskets of assorted warm breads

•

Blueberry-Pear Crisp with Oatmeal (see page 119)
vanilla ice-cream

A Mostly Moroccan Menu

A feast of flavours to brighten any winter evening. Set your table to match: cover with a bright cloth and arrange the food on colourful platters.

mixed cured olives
Moroccan Spiced Carrot Soup (see page 24)
warm flat bread

•

Coriander Roast Lamb with Spiced Chickpea Sauce (see page 71)
Roast Winter Roots (see page 102)
buttered couscous

•

chilled sliced oranges
a winter fruit plate of dried apricots, dried figs and fresh dates

An Intimate Fireside Supper

As the evenings darken and the air turns cold, it's time to ward off the winter blues with this special menu. Candlelight, best china, white linen, and good friends essential.

Watercress, Chicory and Smoked Salmon Salad with Horseradish Dressing (see page 38)

•

Pan-Roast Chicken with Herbed Goat's Cheese (see page 62)
Carrot Smashed Potatoes (see page 94)

•

Chocolate Truffle Torte (see page 124)

Sunday Lunch at Home

A just about all-year round menu that sticks to all the best Sunday lunch traditions, jazzed up with a few new ideas.

Potato, Garlic and Leek Soup (see page 23)

•

Perfect Roast Chicken with Green Olives and Lemon Roast Potatoes (see page 77)
Sizzling Garlic Greens (see page 92)

•

vanilla ice-cream
Chocolate Fudge Topping (see page 116)

A Midsummer Feast for Friends

Set the table in a shady spot in the garden and open a chilled bottle of crisp white or dry rosé.

Bruschetta with Avocado Goat's Cheese
(see page 56)
•
Roast Red Pepper and Tomato Soup
with Basil (see page 26)
•
Grilled Eggplant Pizza with Basil
(see page 50)
a leafy salad of seasonal greens
Lemon Garlic Dressing (see page 108)
•
Luscious Lemon Cheesecake
(see page 123)
ripe strawberries

A Sit-Down Family Brunch for a Winter Weekend

Brunch is the most relaxed of meals and a good choice for a casual family get-together. All the dishes can be prepared well ahead of time and only need a few minutes in the oven to warm through. Mimosas - freshly squeezed orange juice and champagne - complete this classic menu.

Onion Tart (see page 65)
a leafy salad of seasonal greens
Honey Mustard Dressing (see page 108)
•
Lemon Pear Yoghurt Muffins
(see page 138)
Cranberry and Orange Crumble Cake
(see page 127)
a winter fruit bowl of mandarins,
bananas and kiwis
•
coffee, tea

Easy Weekday Suppers

If you fancy a proper sweet and sticky ending, look no further than our quick-fix toppings for vanilla ice-cream - toffee banana, very berry, caramelized apple and chocolate fudge (see page 116).

Spring Supper
Spiced Green Lentil Soup with Spinach
and Lemon (see page 29)
•
yoghurt with sliced banana and
a drizzle of honey

Summer Supper
Red Peppers Stewed with Potatoes and
Olives (see page 92)
•
a fruit plate of sliced peaches and
strawberries

Autumn Supper
Roast Cherry Tomato Spaghetti
(see page 69)
•
ripe pears, walnuts and a wedge of
blue cheese

Winter Supper
Red Lentil Dhal with Aromatics
(see page 82)
steamed rice
•
mandarins

Late Summer Grill Dinner

Backyard barbecue parties are an easy way to entertain. While your guests gather round the grill, let the savoury, smoky aromas set their appetites on fire!

Bruschetta with Avocado Goat's Cheese
(see page 56)
•
Grilled Vegetable Platter with Pesto
Dressing (see page 37)
Grilled Balsamic Lamb Chops
(see page 82)
New Potato Salad with Shallot
Vinaigrette (see page 111)
•
Mini Pavlovas with Summer Berries
(see page 128)

French Farmhouse Feast

Festive fare with a French accent for family and friends. Accompany with a full-bodied red wine and have plenty of bread to hand at all times.

Potato, Garlic and Parsley Soup
(see page 23)
•
French Leek Tart (see page 65)
•
Slow-Simmered Beef Daube with Red
Wine and Garlic (see page 78)
•
country-style bread
French cheese platter
•
Upside Down Apple Caramel Cake
(see page 114)
crème fraîche

It's Springtime!

Celebrate spring with this light luncheon menu that pays homage to the fresh produce of the new season. Rather than using mixed vegetables for the platter, grill tender asparagus spears and choose parsley rather than basil for making the pesto dressing.

Grilled Vegetable Platter with Pesto
Dressing (see pge 37)
•
Spring Vegetable Ragoût (see page 104)
warm crusty bread
•
Strawberry-Rhubarb Crisp with
Oatmeal (see page 119)
thick cream

Index

Index compiled by Sue Bosanko

EDITORIAL CONSULTANT
Rosie Kindersley
DESIGN AND ART DIRECTION
Stuart Jackman
PROJECT EDITOR
Sally Somers
PRODUCTION MANAGER
Maryann Webster

FOOD STYLING
Eric Treuillé

Acknowledgements

Eric Treuillé would like to thank:
As ever, my wife Rosie, for
making it all happen, again.
Julia Pemberton Hellums, for
making sense of it all, again.
The Books for Cooks Team,
especially Victoria Blashford Snell
and Ursula Ferrigno, for their
passion for good food and their
willingness to share their
inspiration with us.
Sally Somers, for the dhal lesson
and for arguing about everything -
both much appreciated.
Ian O'Leary, for fabulous photos,
of course, but also for giving me
the chance to work with a
photographer, rather than just
for one.
Stuart Jackman, for giving us the
opportunity, for being on board,
for making this one so damn
gorgeous.

Renée Elliott would like to thank:
Brian, my husband, for his
unconditional support. My mom,
for celebrating food and cooking.
My dad, for the vegetable garden.
Rosie Kindersley, for bringing it
all together. And Peter, her father,
for making this possible.